Usel
£3
Trav
2041

Awakening Minorities

*tran*saction/**Society** Book Series

Awakening Minorities

American Indians
Mexican Americans, Puerto Ricans

Edited by
JOHN R. HOWARD

ta

Transaction Books
New Brunswick, New Jersey

Transaction Books
Rutgers University
New Brunswick, New Jersey 08903

Library of Congress Catalog Card Number: 70-115942
ISBN: 0-87855-0550 (cloth); 0-87855-548-X (paper)

Printed in the United States of America

Contents

Preface

For the past decade, *trans*action, and now **Society**, has dedicated itself to the task of reporting the strains and conflicts within the American system. But the magazine has done more than this. It has pioneered in social programs for changing the social order, offered the kind of analysis that has permanently restructured the terms of the "dialogue" between peoples and publics, and offered the sort of prognosis that makes for real alterations in economic and political policies directly affecting our lives.

The work done in the magazine has crossed disciplinary boundaries. This represents much more than simple cross-disciplinary "team efforts." It embodies rather a recognition that the social world cannot be easily carved into neat academic disciplines; that, indeed, the study of the experience of blacks in American ghettos, or the manifold uses and abuses of agencies of law enforcement, or the sorts of overseas policies that lead to the celebration of some dictatorships and the condemnation of others, can best be examined from many viewpoints and from the vantage points of many disciplines.

The editors of **Society** magazine are now making available in permanent form the most important work done in the magazine, supplemented in some cases by additional materials edited to reflect the tone and style developed over the years by *trans*action. Like the magazine, this series of books demonstrates the superiority of starting with real world problems and searching out practical solutions, over the zealous guardianship of professional boundaries. Indeed, it is precisely this approach that has elicited enthusiastic support from leading American social scientists, many of whom are represented among the editors of these volumes.

The subject matter of these books concerns social changes and social policies that have aroused the long-standing needs and present-day anxieties of us all. These changes are in organizational lifestyles, concepts of human ability and intelligence, changing patterns of norms and morals, the relationship of social conditions to physical and biological environments, and in the status of social science with respect to national policy making. The editors feel that many of these articles have withstood the test of time, and match in durable interest the best of available social science literature. This collection of essays, then, attempts to address itself to immediate issues without violating the basic insights derived from the classical literature in the various fields of social science.

As the political crises of the sixties have given way to the economic crunch of the seventies, the social scientists involved as editors and authors of this series have gone beyond observation of critical areas, and have entered into the vital and difficult tasks of explanation and interpretation. They have defined issues in a way that makes solutions possible. They have provided answers as well as asked the right questions. These books, based as they are upon the best materials from *trans*action / **Society** magazine, are dedicated to highlighting social problems alone, and beyond that, to establishing guidelines for social solutions based on the social sciences.

The remarkable success of the book series to date is indicative of the need for such "fastbacks" in college course work and, no less, in the everyday needs of busy people who have not surrendered the need to know, nor the lively sense required to satisfy such knowledge needs. It is also plain that what superficially appeared as a random selection of articles on the basis of subject alone, in fact, represented a careful concern for materials that are addressed to issues at the shank and marrow of society. It is the distillation of the best of these, systematically arranged, that appears in these volumes.

THE EDITORS
*trans*action / Society

Ethnic Stratification Systems

JOHN R. HOWARD

All societies stratify their members. Stratification refers to the hierarchical ordering of people. In the American context, ethnic stratification refers to the ranking of categories of people in terms of skin color and/or national origin. Ethnic stratification systems are systems of inequality. They reflect unequal access to goods, services, pleasures, and power. These inequalities are rationalized by belief systems which posit that the dispossessed have brought their problems on themselves through sloth or inate lack of ability.

Most of the literature on racial and ethnic relations in the United States deals either with Negroes or European immigrant groups. There is considerably less on American Indians, Mexican Americans, and Puerto Ricans. Indians have received more attention from social scientists than the other two groups, but most of this literature is ethnographic or historical in nature, the analytic perspectives employed not conceptualizing them as a minority group.

1

It is not at all clear that the explanatory models developed in the study of blacks and European immigrant groups are applicable to these relatively neglected minorities. Much of the literature on black-white relations attempts to account for the persistence of anti-black sentiments by focusing on cognitive processes associated with stereotyping and on the dynamics of the prejudiced personality type. Lately, increased attention has been given to clashes of interest between blacks and whites over control of community resources and institutions such as schools, poverty programs and, in some places, city hall itself. Cultural differences and the assimilation process have been central in the analysis of the experiences of European immigrant groups, the generalization being that acculturation (the manifestation, at least on public occasions, of the style and modes of behavior of the dominant group) decreases hostility toward immigrants and facilitates a certain degree of assimilation.

Neither of these approaches is appropriate as regards Indians, Mexican Americans, and Puerto Ricans. On the one hand, they have not been victimized by the obsessive prejudice directed at blacks; on the other hand, there has been sufficient hostility as to make their status considerably less affirmative than that of European immigrant groups. It cannot be assumed that they will go the way of these groups. While Puerto Ricans are recent immigrants, Indians and a portion of the Mexican-American population have been in the country for a considerable period of time without shedding their minority group status.

If existing analytic approaches are insufficient as regards accounting for the status of these three groups then, of course, we have need for new ones. Below, an alternative perspective is suggested.

Of Partial and Total Minority Groups

The fundamental fact of ethnic stratification is domination of one group by another. Members of minority groups experience stigma on categorical grounds. In other words, irrespective of the individual's attributes or behavior he is subject to stigma by virtue of his group identity. This stigma manifests itself in terms of social exclusion, economic oppression and political powerlessness. Minority group status implies at least these three conditions.

• Social exclusion is expressed in a complex set of sanctions and taboos regulating the manner in which members of the minority group and the majority group may interact. These taboos have in the past extended to barring members of minority groups from places of public accommodation such as restaurants, theaters, parks and beaches. They currently still entail the exercise of formal and informal sanctions on patterns of interpersonal interaction implying equal social status, e.g., membership in the same social clubs or marriage. These patterns of exclusion are rationalized by an elaborate mythology suggesting the degenerate nature of the minority group.

• Economic oppression is a fairly complex matter. On its most obvious level it entails the denial of employment opportunities on categorical grounds. On a less obvious level it bears on the economics of exploitation. Being restricted to low-paying jobs, members of minority groups find, paradoxically, that it costs a lot to be poor. The poor have trouble getting credit at reputable stores and are forced to patronize slum merchants charging exorbitant interest on time-payments for shoddy goods. Having their choices in the housing market limited by discrimination, minority group members pay high rents and high interest rates on mortgage for dwellings inferior in quality to those they otherwise might command.

Recently there has been a revival of a mode of analysis in which ghettoes are conceptualized as exploited domestic colonies. Carey McWilliams used this approach during the 1940s. It has lately been rediscovered by some younger social scientists and political radicals. The ghetto as an exploited domestic colony is seen as a place with shrunken, inadequately financed, and poorly functioning institutions —schools that do not educate, hospitals in disrepair, transportation systems of great insufficiency.

Exploitation is a self-reinforcing phenomenon. Groups that are exploited economically find themselves without the wherewithal to further exploitation.

• The minority group lacks the power by itself to significantly improve its condition. Its powerlessness may derive from formal restrictions on the opportunity to participate in politics (literacy tests, for example) or from informal sanctions (for example, night rider terror). Additionally, institutionalized political arrangements such as gerrymandering may mute their potential for political effectiveness.

The minority group has subordinate status, but not all minority groups have the same status. All are unequal, but some are less unequal than others.

American Indians, Mexican Americans, and Puerto Ricans have a status distinct from that of blacks. They are not as visible, and outside of areas in which they are concentrated geographically, the disabilities visited upon them are not as pervasive as those visited upon blacks. They are what might be termed "partial minorities."

Several characteristics identify the partial minority group. Domination of one group by another is the essence of ethnic stratification, but the style of domination differs as do partial and total minority groups.

At least three styles of domination can be identified: class domination; what, for want of a better term, might be called "semi-caste" domination; and caste domination.

Class domination refers to situations where a group's subordinate status is a consequence of the fact that the group is poor and most of its members foreign. As the group loses its foreignness and becomes mobile, or, as it becomes mobile and loses its foreignness, hostility toward it decreases. This was the experience of most European immigrant groups. It was never the case, of course, that European immigrant groups simply disappeared into the melting pot. Consciousness of ethnic identity persists. Bailey and Katz in *Ethnic Group Politics* indicate "that ethnic group identification is real can be seen in many . . . forms. Numerous agencies are organized by nationality groups as well as racial and religious groups. Second, the existence of ethnic group identification can be seen in the large numbers of foreign language publications in the United States estimated to have a circulation over ten million. Third, ethnic groups carry on a great many 'separate' social activities . . . in a single weekend in New York separate dances for persons of Hungarian, Irish, Italian, German and Polish extraction are advertised in the neighborhood newspapers and foreign language press. Finally . . . ethnic groups behave in distinctive ways in the American political system."

Ethnic identity persists, then, among European immigrant groups, but mutual hostility based on ethnic group identity has receded.

Semi-caste domination refers to a situation where a group itself is regarded as unacceptable, but exceptions are made for individuals who adopt the style and manner of the dominant group. Systematic impediments to group mobility are imposed by the dominant population, but individuals who manage to acquire the education, manner and outlook of the dominant group are defined as members of the dominant group. The major difference between this mode of domination and class domination lies in the existence of more rigid barriers to collective mobility. This mode of domination has characterized relations between dominant groups and partial minorities.

The status of partial minority groups in the United States is analogous, in certain respects, to that of blacks in Brazil and Puerto Rico. There has been a good deal of confused discussion in the literature over the nature of prejudice in Latin America. It has been recognized, on the one hand, that the obsessive malevolence which has characterized attitudes toward blacks in the United States does not find a counterpart in Latin America, but on the other hand, Latin Americans are not free of color prejudice. Blacks cluster at the lower end of the class ladder and strong barriers exist to collective mobility. They are the objects of class hostility and color prejudice. If a black is mobile in class terms, however, he is put into an exemption category and becomes "white" for many social purposes. Shibutani and Kwan observed that "In Brazil . . . Darkness is still reminiscent of slave origins, but it can be compensated for by other qualities. Although darker people are still concentrated in the lower classes . . . many persons of unmistakable African ancestry are classified as Branco and are so treated by their associates. One population expression is that 'a rich Negro is a white man, and a poor white man is a Negro'."

Somewhat the same is true in the United States with regard to American Indians, Mexican Americans, and Puerto Ricans. Most are poor and are the objects of class and ethnic hostility. The structure of opportunities is not adequate to afford mobility to any significant percentage of each group, but where a member of any of these groups exhibits the style and manner of the dominant group he may escape the indignities otherwise visited upon members of the group and may be regarded as a member of the dominant group. This phenomenon is dealt with at length in the Wahrhaftig and Thomas article in this book on the Cherokee Indians in Oklahoma, and in the essay introducing the articles on Mexican Americans.

Caste domination occurs when the barriers between the dominant group and the minority are regarded as ultimately impermeable. Caste has been defined by the sociologist Joseph Himes as a "type of social organization composed of ranked, mutually exclusive units between which virtually no social mobility is permitted." In the American context blacks have had a caste-like position. Historically, their position has been one of rigid social exclusion, ruthless exploitation, and political powerlessness, all supported by law, sentiment, and the knout. The civil rights struggle has modified the position of blacks, but their place relative to that of the partial minorities probably remains unchanged.

The key factor differentiating this category from the semi-caste category is the assumed indelible character of caste. Implicitly, in popular thinking black ancestry constitutes an indelible genetic stain which can never be entirely removed. This is symbolized in beliefs with regard to ancestry and black identity. Any person with known black ancestry is thought of as black, however "white" he may be phenotypically, whereas an individual with equally slight Indian ancestry is not thought of as "Indian." The concept of "passing" is based on the assumption that an individual who is phenotypically white but has some remote black ancestry *is* black. On the other hand, a person with equally remote Indian or Mexican ancestry would not be regarded as passing, as hiding his *true* group identity.

The essence of caste domination is that a group is outside the system of rights, privileges, and immunities believed proper for ordinary people. They occupy a special subordinate position with highly circumscribed opportunities for mobility in social class terms. Their special genetic taint is believed irradicable. It is assumed that there is something about "Negroness" that cannot be washed away. (The average man does not have literal beliefs about "genes," of course, but his position translates metaphorically into the proposition stated here.)

The position of the partial minority group is sustained, in part, by geographical concentration and small numbers. American Indians, Mexican Americans, and Puerto Ricans concentrate heavily in certain parts of the country. Outside the areas in which each concentrates most persons are not sensitive, at the interpersonal level, to the symbols of their group identity. In other words, while the San Antonio businessman is likely to be sensitive to certain elements of style and appearance which identify a person as Mexican American and to have stereotypes of Mexican behavior, the Syracuse businessman is not. The Mexican American applying for employment might be mistaken for Italian or Greek, or possibly Puerto Rican. The Syracuse businessman is less likely to have strongly held stereotypes of Mexicans and to treat a given Mexican as a member of a minority group. The black, however, in an interactional sense, is a member of a minority group in both San Antonio and Syracuse.

The position of the partial minority group is paradoxical. By being somewhat below the threshold of public consciousness with regard to "minority problems" they escape some of the pervasive indignities visited upon blacks, but, precisely because of this it becomes difficult to arouse public indignation at the depredations they do suffer. As some of the articles in this book indicate, it also creates problems for them as regards defining and understanding their own status.

The American social system is very complex. It is interlaced with a dozen or more ethnic and racial categories crosscut by several strata of social class. The processes whereby groups come to occupy given positions is as complex as the system itself. These processes are the subject of the essays which introduce the readings on each group. This book is divided into three sections, one on each group. Most of the articles deal with their contemporary problems and status. The purpose of the introductory essays is to provide an historical context against which the articles can be better understood. The introductory essays attempt to present both a chronology of events and an elucidation of the processes those events reflected. Minority groups are made, not born, and the introductory essays tell how. The essays and the articles together do, I trust, present a clear picture of these Awakening Minorities.

American Indians: Goodby to Tonto

JOHN R. HOWARD

It is the fate of American Indians that they exist in the national consciousness mainly as figures in a myth of the American past. Black writer James Baldwin's observation that "nobody knows my name" applies equally to Indians. Ralph Ellison's "invisible man" is the Indian as well as the black man. His mythical essence is more than his contemporary existence.

In the American psyche, Indians have fulfilled their historical mission. They existed to provide a human challenge to whites as they marched across the continent. Their resistance provided the stuff of myths of conquest and glory. Winthrop Jordan, the historian, commented in *Black Over White* on the symbolic meaning of the Indian in American experience in the 18th and 19th centuries. "Confronting the Indian in America was a testing experience, common to all the colonies. Conquering the Indian symbolized and personified the conquest of the American difficulties, the

11

surmounting of the wilderness. To push back the Indian was to prove the worth of one's own mission, to make straight in the desert a highway of civilisation."

For many Americans there is something faintly anachronistic about contemporary Indians. One looks at them as figures out of the past, as relics of a more heroic age. Put somewhat differently, their existence has been hard to grasp. It is only recently that they have begun to make their special presence known.

This essay briefly describes the contemporary position of the Indian and recounts the sequence of historical events which have brought him to this place.

American Indians Today

Just how many Indians there are in the United States is unclear. The 1960 census placed the figure at just over half a million, but Vine Deloria, former executive director of the National Congress of American Indians, estimates the number at closer to one million. There is also disagreement as to the number of Indians on reservations. The 1960 census reported 243,412, while Deloria, and Robert Sherrill in his work on the Pine Ridge Sioux, speak of close to 400,000. Disagreements about the total number are partly a consequence of problems of definition. What degree of Indian ancestry makes one an Indian? Unfortunately there are no data that allow us to differentiate clearly among persons of mixed ancestry in terms of those who identify themselves as Indian and those who do not.

Whatever the disagreement about numbers, all parties are in accord that Indians have the sad distinction of being the most depressed of America's racial and ethnic groups. Sherrill has observed that "No minority group in this country is as poor as the 380,000 or so Indians who live on reservations. The average family income for Indians is said to be about $1,500, but the average on-reservation income is much lower. Unemployment ranges from 45 percent to 98 percent, the latter being the winter rate on some of the Dakota reservations." The Bureau of Indian Affairs estimates that 71 percent of reservation Indians live in inadequate housing. The infant mortality rate seems consistently to be two to three times that of the rest of the population. Records compiled by the University of Colorado School of Medicine indicated a rate of 88.2 deaths per 1,000 live births among the Utes in 1960. Sherrill described the large Pine Ridge reservation visited by the late Robert Kennedy. "In housing, employment and life style, the 10,000 to 12,000 Sioux . . . on the Pine Ridge Reservation are still untouched by the benevolence of Washington. A few families are living in abandoned auto bodies. Some families live in tents, some in abandoned chicken coops. . . . At least 75 percent of the dwellings on this reservation have no plumbing." The life expectancy of a reservation Indian is 46 years, more than two decades less than that of whites and considerably less than blacks.

Indians are most heavily concentrated in the Southwest, with over 100,000 living in Arizona and New Mexico. Another 64,000 live in Oklahoma. Numerous smaller communities and tribes are found in California, Oregon, and Washington, and in the north central states: North Dakota, Minnesota, Wisconsin, and Michigan. Other groupings are found in New York, North Carolina, Rhode Island, and other states.

In a sense, the essence of the Indians' problem is that they lack the power to act in their own behalf. Their powerlessness derives in part from lack of numbers, and in part from their unique legal status. Indians are citizens, the Indian Citizens Act of 1924 having conferred full constitutional rights on all Indians who were not then citizens. Their collective, tribal rights are also defined by certain treaties, however, and they are subject, in certain respects, to the Bureau of Indian Affairs. The Bureau of Indian Affairs acts within a framework of powers defined by Congress; and Congress has from time to time enacted legislation which has been devastating in terms of Indian interests.

Blacks are the only other racial or ethnic group in the United States to have been subject to special legislation, but the concept of "equal protection" of the laws has resulted in the rescinding of anti-black legislation. The Indian's dual citizenship has left him subject to legislation having such possibilities. While Indians are citizens, they are also dealt with, insofar as tribal lands and tribal rights are concerned, as members of a conquered nation whose rights can be expanded, contracted, or otherwise modified as the conqueror sees fit.

Recent years have witnessed a rise in Indian militancy. Deloria, a Standing Rock Sioux, articulated the Indian's position in *Custer Died for Your Sins.* In locales with large Indian populations there are bumper stickers bearing testimony to the new spirit: "Indians Discovered America," "Indian Power," "Custer Had it Coming ." The fairly complicated situation and protest of the Indian is made easier to grasp by placing it in historical context. Let us then briefly recount the sequence of events which yielded the present state of affairs.

The Changing Status of American Indians

As it has for blacks, the majority society has from time to time asked itself what to do with, about, or to American

Indians. Farb has observed that "Two contrasting images of the Indian—as Noble Red Man and as Blood Thirsty Savage—have prevailed in the minds of whites in the past five hundred years, and feelings have tended to shift back and forth between the two." In recent decades Indians have been either ignored or viewed as the special concern of people given to exotic causes, the country and western singer Johnny Cash, for example, being known to have a "thing" about convicts and Indians.

No national policy on Indians existed prior to the end of the 18th century as no (white) American nation existed; and neither did Indians as a political or social collectivity exist. Just as European colonial powers imposed a collective national identity on disparate African peoples, so the collective identity of Indians derives from their common experience of defeat and mistreatment at the hands of Americans.

The first century and a half of European-Indian contact along the eastern seaboard presents a confused picture. Some tribes greeted the newcomers with friendship, others vacillated between hostility and friendship. Intertribal relations were characterized by shifting alliances and periodic wars between longstanding enemies. Indians seeking to even old scores with other tribes or gain material advantage often allied themselves with colonists in their battles with hostile tribes. A series of violent encounters accompanied the settlement of the colonies. The Pequots of the Connecticut Valley were massacred in 1637, the Swamp Fight occurred in Rhode Island in 1675, and Bloody Brook in Massachusetts the same year. The Tuscarora of North Carolina were defeated in 1713 and the Yamasee of South Carolina in 1715. Gradually the tribes lost effective control over their own lands.

A turning point of Indian policy, an event which defined the status Indians were to have in the new nation, occurred with the expropriation of the Cherokees' land. From the perspective of the Indians there had always been the problem of how to adapt to the penetration of Europeans. A few chose to fight, others, seeking advantage over rivals, entered into temporary alliances with the newcomers, assuming implicitly that the coming of Europeans would entail no fundamental change in their traditional way of life. As the reality of European domination became unequivocal the Cherokee chose to adopt the ways of the conqueror.

About 1790 the Cherokees decided to modify their traditional culture. They established churches, schools, and well-cultivated farms. Farb reports that "In 1826 a Cherokee reported to the Presbyterian Church that his people already possessed 22,000 cattle, 7,600 houses, 46,000 swine, 2,500 sheep, 762 looms, 1,488 spinning wheels, 2,948 plows, 10 saw mills, 31 grist mills, 62 blacksmith shops, and 18 schools. In one of the Cherokee districts alone there were some 1,000 volumes 'of good books'. In 1821 . . . a Cherokee named Sequoyah . . . perfected a method of syllabary notation in which English letters stood for Cherokee syllables; by 1828 the Cherokee were already publishing their own newspaper. At about the same time they adopted a written constitution providing for an executive, a bicameral legislature, a supreme court, and a code of laws."

In a theoretical sense the Cherokee constitute a crucial case. To what extent would the society accommodate itself to Indians who were "just like everyone else"? The answer was, not at all. The Cherokee were unable to save themselves even by adopting what, from the majority perspective, should have been viewed as exemplary values.

White demands for Indian lands created pressure for

their removal. The Cherokee were simply one of a number of tribes to be moved west of the Mississippi. On December 19, 1829, the Georgia state legislature passed an act appropriating a large area of the Cherokee nation. Georgia only reflected the mood in Washington. Farb indicates that ". . . President Jackson had been reared on the frontier and he was utterly insensitive to the treatment of the Indians. He denounced as an 'absurdity' and a 'farce' that the United States should bother even to negotiate treaties with Indians as if they were independent nations with a right to their lands. He was completely in sympathy with the policy of removal of Indians to new lands west of the Mississippi. He exerted his influence to make Congress give legal sanction to what in our time, under the Nuremberg Laws, would be branded as genocide. Dutifully Congress passed the Removal Act of 1830, which gave the President the right to extirpate all Indians who had managed to survive east of the Mississippi River."

Again some tribes chose to fight. The Seminoles of Florida resisted from 1835 to 1842, costing the United States some 1,500 troops and $20,000,000. "Many of the Iroquois sought sanctuary in Canada, and the Oneida and the Seneca were moved westward, although fragments of Iroquois tribes managed to remain behind in western New York. The Sac and Fox made a desperate stand in Illinois . . . but ultimately their survivors were forced to move as were the Ottawa, Potawatomie, Wyandot, Shawnee, Kickapoo, Winnebago, Delaware, Peioria, Miami and many others who are remembered now only in the name of some town, lake, county or state, or as a footnote in the annals of a local history society."

The Cherokee appealed to Washington but eventually were uprooted and forced west over the thousand-mile "trail of tears." An estimate made at the time stated that 4,000 died en route. In terms of the position developed in the introductory essay the Cherokee were subjected to caste oppression. Their high degree of cultural and physical visibility sustained a body of perjorative myth which served to rationalize what was clearly the grossest violation of their rights.

The fate of the Cherokee and other tribes forced west reflected a policy of confining Indians to tracts of land on the western plains. But white migration inevitably created pressure for more and more expropriation of reservation lands.

Greed for Indian lands, and a sympathy for Indians expressed as the desire to encourage their assimilation, came together to produce the Dawes Act of 1887. In a sense it marks the beginning of the modern era as regards relations between Indians and the larger society. Indians are still suffering from its tragic consequences.

The period immediately preceding passage of the Dawes Act marked the last stand of the Indians. It is the period celebrated in innumerable cowboy movies. The Sioux rose in 1876, the Nez Perce in 1877, the Cheyenne in 1878 and the Apache in the 1880s, until Geronimo with 36 survivors finally surrendered to General George Crook. A way of life had disappeared and what was to replace it was not clear. White land hunger was unabated and a movement started among some people sympathetic to the Indian "to give the remnant of Indian populations the dignity of private property . . . the plan was widely promoted in the halls of Congress, in the press and in the meetings of religious societies." Senator Henry L. Dawes, the Act's sponsor, hoped it might salvage something for the Indians. Unfortunately, it had loopholes which also made it attractive to those coveting Indian territory.

The Dawes Act authorized the President to parcel out tribal lands to individual Indians, each adult to receive 160 acres and each minor child 80 acres. The argument was that if given his own plot of land, the Indian could become an industrious farmer. Whatever acreage was left over was to be declared "surplus" and offered for sale to whites, the proceeds presumably to be spent by the Department of the Interior for the benefit of Indians.

Some tribes resisted allotment and the Creeks, Choctaws, Chickasaws, Cherokees, Seminoles, and several others were exempted. The Act failed to break up tribes or convert Indians into farmers; instead it resulted in the impoverishment of much of the Indian population. Between 1887 and 1932 approximately 90 million acres out of 138 million initially held by Indians passed to white ownership. Josephy observed that ". . . much of the land allotted to them was too poor to farm, and they received no financial credit nor little help of any other kind. Many Indians totally estranged from non-Indian economic motivations and customs, leased or sold their lands to whites at bargain prices; others were swindled out of their holdings; and poverty, drunkenness, and debauchery increased."

"Indians who sold their land," Deloria states, "did not merge into white society and disappear. They simply moved onto their relatives' lands and remained within the tribal society. Thus the land base was diminishing while the population continued to remain constant and, in some cases, grew spectacularly."

The rapid decline of Indians was finally halted with the passage in 1934 of the Wheeler-Howard Act, better known as the Indian Reorganization Act. This legislation grew out of investigations of Indian conditions in 1926. The

Indian Reorganization Act tacitly acknowledged that assimilation was still far off. It ended the allotment policy,
encouraged the reformation of tribal government, im-
proved social services on tribal lands and restored freedom
of religion for Indians. The Act sought to let the Indian
use his own culture.

"The Indian response to the new rights and responsi-
bilities was generally slow;" Foreman comments, "after so
many years of wardship, most tribes could not easily adjust
to the new policy. Nevertheless tribal governments were
formed, Indian inhibitions and fears began to disappear,
the initiative and energies of the people began to stir, and
conditions started gradually to improve."

The early 1950s brought another attempt to enforce
assimilation and new hardship to certain tribes. The principle piece of legislation was a resolution declaring Congress' intent to terminate Federal relations with the tribes
at the earliest possible time. The legislation was spurred
by cries that the reservations were havens for the irresponsible and a burden on taxpayers.

Termination proved to be a disaster for those tribes
which felt its impact. First, it lent itself to several interpretations. It could mean the transfer to the federal government of certain services performed by the Bureau of
Indian Affairs; the B.I.A. Division of Health, for example,
giving way to the United States Public Health Service. It
could mean the transfer of Indian students to public schools.
It could mean the extension of the criminal and civil laws
of the state to the reservation, thereby depriving tribes of
substantial powers of local government.

In its most grievous form it entailed the appropriation
of Indian assets. Four bands of Paiutes were the first whose
relations with the B.I.A. were terminated and their expe-

riences bode ill for those Indians to whom the law was to be applied. The Shivwits, Koosharem, Indian Peaks, and Kanosh bands of the Paiutes held approximately 46,000 acres of land. They were terminated in 1957 and a year or so later, after their already desperate circumstances had become even worse, they were asked why they had agreed to it in the first place. A Kanosh man indicated that at the time of the hearings they had not understood what was happening. The low educational level of the bands and their general poverty testified to the validity of his assertion. Upon termination, Paiute land was transferred from the Bureau of Indian Affairs to trustees of the Walker Bank and Trust Company in Salt Lake City, 160 miles away. Aberle and Brophy recount that "The Paiutes had difficulty getting transportation to the bank and then communicating with the trust officer. An Indian Peaks man said that they finally collected enough money for gasoline to go to Salt Lake City, where they saw the trustee, but they could not understand his remarks and after a few minutes were shown out of his office. They also tried unsuccessfully to get advice from an attorney appointed by the bank and paid with Paiute money. Later the attorney wrote the Indian Peaks official that he would have samples of valuable minerals found on tribal land tested. 'But,' the Paiute continued, 'we do not know one stone from another.'"

Basically, the Paiutes were cast forth and told to survive. They had neither the resources nor the experience. Sending their children to public school entailed a $15 a year activity fee per child and one dollar a week for school lunch, expenses they could not meet. They could not pay doctor or hospital bills. The very circumstances of their old life denied the possibility of easy survival under the new system: lacking birth certificates and social security numbers because they had not been needed, they had difficulty obtaining social services following withdrawal of certain forms of B.I.A. assistance.

Termination had the same unhappy consequences for the relatively well-off Menominee as it had for the already impoverished Paiutes. The Menominees owned a forest in Wisconsin and operated a sawmill to provide employment for tribal members. Deloria described the affects of termination. "Termination of Federal Supervision meant an immediate tax bill of 55 percent on the sawmill. To meet this, the sawmill had to be automated, thus throwing a substantial number of Indians out of work and onto the unemployment rolls. To meet the rising unemployment situation, the only industry, the sawmill, had to be taxed by the county. There was an immediate spiral downward in the capital structure of the tribe so that in the years since the termination bill was passed, it has had to receive some $10 million in special state and Federal aid. The end is not yet in sight."

Rising Indian protest brought an end to implementation of termination during the Kennedy and Johnson years, although it still, presumably, remains the intent of Congress. The War on Poverty brought a variety of new programs to Indian tribes and in many instances involved Indians in decision-making capacities with regard to the kinds of programs a reservation would have and how they were to be run.

Perhaps inspired by the "black power" and "brown power" movements, Indians are now attempting to formulate a set of goals for their people; they are attempting both to define themselves as Indians and to work out a coherent and effective set of strategies for acquiring sufficient political power to act on their own behalf.

Indian Power: What it Means

With the end of the plains wars between the last independent Indian tribes and the United States Army a different kind of "Indian problem" faced the nation. It was no longer a matter of seizing and holding Indian lands but rather of working out a policy toward a conquered people. Those favoring termination of the reservations, whether under the Dawes Act, or several decades later under the House resolution, assumed, implicitly, that there would be no Indian problem if there were no Indians. Legislation to force assimilation had the consequence, however, of eroding the resources of those Indians who remained on the reservations without providing assistance to those pushed out from under the domain of the B.I.A. In other words, they yielded to Indians the worst of both worlds. Thus, the Indian today is the nation's most depressed ethnic group.

An increasing number of Indians are demanding "Indian Power." The program associated with Indian power seems to entail roughly the following:

First, Indians resolve the dilemma of dual citizenship by wanting the best of both worlds. They desire to retain reservations as bases from which to develop. By developing the reservations in whatever terms seem to make economic sense, they seek some degree of economic independence, and hopefully even affluence. They are motivated to retain their land not only out of the knowledge that it is all that is left to them of a continent they once owned, but possibly out of the intuitive, but nevertheless correct perception, that without the land their resources are nil, and they become like the dust of the plains, blown here and there with no place their own.

They seek however to change the terms under which they have held the land. They have been treated as wards in both legal fact and administrative reality. The Great White Father has assumed that his Indian children were incompetent to run their own affairs. Indians desire all the services they can get from the federal government, but they also want to make their own decisions with regard to how these services and resources can best be used in the interests of the Indian community.

Anglos might question the propriety of this approach: "They want to have their cake and eat it too." The unspoken Indian response is, "You made us what we are today—poor, untutored, dependent—you should help us become something else."

Second, Indians desire to retain their identity as Indians. Retention of tribal lands seems to be both a strategic matter relating to an enhanced standard of living and an affirmation of Indian identity. In a sense, this is more important than the materialist issue. Indians were defeated by Europeans not only militarily and politically but also psychologically. The hypothesized negative self-image of blacks, extirpated by the cultural nationalism of the black power movement has its analogue in the shattered ego of Indians, "drunken redskins," "bloodthirsty savages," "gifted makers of beads and trinkets," expunged by the Indian power movement. It is not a law of nature that Tonto must ride in the Lone Ranger's shadow. Implicitly, the supporters of termination deny the value of Indian culture and the validity of the contemporary Indian's historically derived and probably unique perspective. They deny that the communalism expressed in the tribal holding of land is worth retaining. For an Indian to support this is to agree that the Indian has fulfilled his historical purpose and is "no longer needed." The implicit, and probably growing, cultural nationalism of the Indian power movement asserts the value of Indian culture and seeks the survival of Indians as an identifiable people.

FURTHER READING

The Indian: America's Unfinished Business by William Brophy and Sophie Brophy (Norman: University of Oklahoma Press, 1966). An excellent discussion of the complex of laws which bear on Indians and of recent Indian policy.

Man's Rise to Civilisation by Peter Farb (New York: E.P. Dutton and Company, Inc., 1968). The best and most readable general treatment on Indians now in print.

The Nez Perce Indians and the Opening of the Northwest by Alvin Josephy (New Haven, Yale University Press, 1965) competent scholarship but a rather specialized topic.

The Five Civilised Tribes by Grant Foreman (Norman: University of Oklahoma Press, 1966). A first rate history of the Cherokees and the other so-called 'civilised tribes.'

On the Border With Crook by John G. Bourne (New York: Charles Scribner, 1892). A colorful though not always credible recounting of the border wars against the last of the Indian tribes resisting the white man, including Geronimo and the Apache.

Custer Died for Your Sins by Vine Deloria (New York: MacMillan, 1969). An account of the relationship of Indians to the white man by an Indian.

"Red Man's Heritage: The Lagoon of Excrement" by Robert G. Sherrill (*The Nation,* Nov. 10, 1969). Contemporary muckraking.

The New Indians by Stan Steiner (New York: Harper and Row, 1968). (The best book thusfar on the 'Red Power Movement.') a radical persuation, by an old-time radical and community

The Warrior Dropouts

ROSALIE H. WAX

A NOTE ON THE STUDY

In studying the adolescents on Pine Ridge we concentrated on two areas, the high school and a particular day school community with a country Indian population of about 1,000. We interviewed somewhat less than half the young people then enrolled in the high school plus a random sample of 48 young country Indians. Subsequently, we obtained basic socio-economic and educational data from all the young people who had graduated from the day school in 1961, 1962, and 1963. We interviewed 153 young people between the ages of 13 and 21, about 50 of whom were high school dropouts. We used many approaches and several types of questionnaires, but our most illuminating and reliable data were obtained from interviews conducted by Indian college students who were able to associate with the Sioux adolescents and participate in some of their activities.

While "country Sioux" or "country Indian" might loosely be considered a synonym for "full-blood," I have avoided the latter term as connoting a traditional Indian culture which vanished long ago and whose unchanging qualities were a mythology of white observers rather than a social reality of Indian participants. In any case, I use "country Indian" to refer to the people raised and

27

living "out on the reservation (prairie)" who participate in the social and ceremonial activities of their local rural communities, as opposed to those persons, also known as Indians, who live in Pine Ridge town and make a point of avoiding these backwoods activities.

Scattered over the prairie on the Pine Ridge reservation of South Dakota, loosely grouped into bands along the creeks and roads, live thousands of Sioux Indians. Most live in cabins, some in tents, a few in houses; most lack the conventional utilities—running water, electricity, telephone, and gas. None has a street address. They are called "country Indians" and most speak the Lakota language. They are very poor, the most impoverished people on the reservation.

For four years I have been studying the problems of the high school dropouts among these Oglala Sioux. In many ways these Indian youths are very different from slum school dropouts—Negro, Mexican-American, rural white —just as in each group individuals differ widely one from another. Yet no one who has any familiarity with their problems can avoid being struck by certain parallels, both between groups and individuals.

In slum schools and Pine Ridge schools scholastic achievement is low, and the dropout rate is high; the children's primary loyalties go to friends and peers, not schools or educators; and all of them are confronted by teachers who see them as inadequately prepared, uncultured offspring of alien and ignorant folk. They are classified as "culturally deprived." All such schools serve as the custodial, constabulary, and reformative arm of one element of society directed against another.

Otherwise well-informed people, including educators themselves, assume on the basis of spurious evidence that dropouts dislike and voluntarily reject school, that they all leave it for much the same reasons, and that they are really much alike. But dropouts leave high school under strikingly different situations and for quite different reasons.

Many explicitly state that they do not wish to leave and are really "pushouts" or "kickouts" rather than "dropouts." As a Sioux youth in our sample put it, "I quit, but I never did *want* to quit!" Perhaps the fact that educators consider all dropouts to be similar tells us more about educators and their schools than about dropouts.

The process that alienates many country Indian boys from the high schools they are obliged to attend begins early in childhood and reflects the basic Sioux social structure. Sioux boys are reared to be physically reckless and impetuous. One that does not perform an occasional brash act may be accepted as "quiet" or "bashful," but he is not considered a desirable son, brother, or sweetheart. Sioux boys are reared to be proud and feisty and are expected to resent public censure. They have some obligations to relatives; but the major social controls after infancy are exerted by their fellows—their "peer group."

From about the age of seven or eight, they spend almost the entire day without adult supervision, running or riding about with friends of their age and returning home only for food and sleep. Even we (my husband, Dr. Murray L. Wax, and I), who had lived with Indian families from other tribal groups, were startled when we heard a responsible and respected Sioux matron dismiss a lad of six or seven for the entire day with the statement, "Go play with Larry and John." Similarly, at a ceremonial gathering in a strange community with hundreds of people, boys of nine or ten often take off and stay away until late at night as a matter of course. Elders pay little attention. There is much prairie and many creeks for roaming and playing in ways that bother nobody. The only delinquencies we have heard Sioux elders complain about are chasing stock, teasing bulls, or occasionally some petty theft.

Among Sioux males this kind of peer-group raising leads to a highly efficient yet unverbalized system of intra-group discipline and powerful intra-group loyalties and dependencies. During our seven-month stay in a reservation community, we were impressed by how rarely the children quarreled with one another. This behavior was not imposed by elders but by the children themselves.

For example, our office contained some items very attractive to them, especially a typewriter. We were astonished to see how quietly they handled this prize that only one could enjoy at a time. A well-defined status system existed so that a child using the typewriter at once gave way and left the machine if one higher in the hierarchy appeared. A half-dozen of these shifts might take place within an hour; yet, all this occurred without a blow or often even a word.

Sioux boys have intense loyalties and dependencies. They almost never tattle on each other. But when forced to live with strangers, they tend to become inarticulate, psychologically disorganized, or withdrawn.

With most children the peer group reaches the zenith of its power in school. In middle class neighborhoods, independent children can usually seek and secure support from parents, teachers, or adult society as a whole. But when, as in an urban slum or Indian reservation, the teachers stay aloof from parents, and parents feel that teachers are a breed apart, the peer group may become so powerful that the children literally take over the school. Then group activities are carried on in class—jokes, notes, intrigues, teasing, mock-combat, comic book reading, courtship—all without the teacher's knowledge and often without grossly interfering with the learning process.

Competent and experienced teachers can come to terms with the peer group and manage to teach a fair amount of reading, writing, and arithmetic. But teachers who are incompetent, overwhelmed by large classes, or sometimes merely inexperienced may be faced with groups of children who refuse even to listen.

We marveled at the variety and efficiency of the devices developed by Indian children to frustrate formal learning—unanimous inattention, refusal to go to the board, writing on the board in letters less than an inch high, inarticulate responses, and whispered or pantomime teasing of victims called on to recite. In some seventh and eighth grade classes there was a withdrawal so uncompromising that no voice could be heard for hours except the teacher's, plaintively asking questions or giving instructions.

Most Sioux children insist they like school, and most Sioux parents corroborate this. Once the power and depth of their social life within the school is appreciated, it is not difficult to see why they like it. Indeed, the only unpleasant aspects of school for them are the disciplinary regulations (which they soon learn to tolerate or evade), an occasional "mean" teacher, bullies, or feuds with members of other groups. Significantly, we found that notorious truants had usually been rejected by classmates and also had no older relatives in school to protect them from bullies. But the child who has a few friends or an older brother or sister to stand by him, or who "really likes to play basketball," almost always finds school agreeable.

By the time he has finished the eighth grade, the country Indian boy has many fine qualities: zest for life, curiosity, pride, physical courage, sensibility to human relationships, experience with the elemental facts of life, and intense group loyalty and integrity. His experiences in day school have done nothing to diminish or tarnish his ideal—the physically reckless and impetuous youth, who is admired by all.

But, on the other hand, the country Indian boy is almost completely lacking in the traits most highly valued by the school authorities: a narrow and absolute respect for "regulations," "government property," routine, discipline, and diligence. He is also deficient in other skills apparently essential to rapid and easy passage through high school and boarding school—especially the abilities to make short-term superficial social adjustments with strangers. Nor can he easily adjust to a system which demands, on the one hand, that he study competitively as an individual, and, on the other, that he live in barrack-type dormitories where this kind of study is impossible.

Finally, his English is inadequate for high school work. Despite eight or more years of formal training in reading and writing, many day school graduates cannot converse fluently in English even among themselves. In contrast, most of the students with whom they will compete in higher schools have spoken English since childhood.

To leave home and the familiar and pleasant day school for boarding life at the distant and formidable high school is a prospect both fascinating and frightening. To many young country Indians the agency town of Pine Ridge is a center of sophistication. It has blocks of Indian Bureau homes with lawns and fences, a barber shop, big grocery stores, churches, gas stations, a drive-in confectionary, and even a restaurant with a juke box. While older siblings or cousins may have reported that at high school "they make you study harder," that "they just make you move every minute," or that the "mixed-bloods" or "children of bureau employees" are "mean" or "snotty," there are the compensatory highlights of movies, basketball games, and the social (white man's) dances.

For the young men there is the chance to play high school basketball, baseball, or football; for the young women there is the increased distance from over-watchful, conservative parents. For both, there is the freedom, taken or not, to hitchhike to White Clay, with its beer joints, bowling hall, and archaic aura of Western wickedness. If, then, a young man's close friends or relatives decide to go to high school, he will usually want to go too rather than remain at home, circumscribed, "living off his folks." Also, every year, more elders coax, tease, bribe, or otherwise pressure the young men into "making a try" because "nowadays only high school graduates get the good jobs."

The student body of the Oglala Community High School is very varied. First, there are the children of the town dwellers, who range from well-paid white and Indian government employees who live in neat government housing developments to desperately poor people who live in tar paper shacks. Second, there is the large number of institutionalized children who have been attending the Oglala Community School as boarders for the greater part of their lives. Some are orphans, others come from isolated sections of the reservation where there are no day schools, others come from different tribal areas.

But these town dwellers and boarders share an advantage—for them entry into high school is little more than a shift from eighth to ninth grade. They possess an intimate knowledge of their classmates and a great deal of local know-how. In marked contrast, the country Indian freshman enters an alien environment. Not only is he ignorant of how to buck the rules, he doesn't even know the rules. Nor does he know anybody to put him wise.

Many country Indians drop out of high school before they have any clear idea what high school is all about. In our sample, 35 percent dropped out before the end of the ninth grade and many of these left during the first semester. Our first interviews with them were tantalizingly contradictory—about half the young men seemed to have found high school so painful they could scarcely talk about it; the other half were also laconic, but insisted that they had liked school. In time, those who had found school unbearable confided that they had left school because they were lonely or because they were abused by more experienced boarders. Only rarely did they mention that they had trouble with their studies.

The following statement, made by a mild and pleasant boy, conveys some idea of the agony of loneliness, embarrassment, and inadequacy that a country Indian newcomer may suffer when he enters high school:

At day school it was kind of easy for me. But high school was really hard, and I can't figure out even simple questions that they ask me. . . . Besides I'm so quiet [modest and unaggressive] that the boys really took advantage of me. They borrow money from me every Sunday night and they don't even care to pay it back. . . . I can't talk English very good, and I'm really bashful and shy, and I get scared when I talk to white people. I usually just stay quiet in the [day school] classroom, and the teachers will leave me alone. But at boarding school they wanted me to get up and talk or say something. . . . I quit and I never went back. . . . I can't seem to get along with different people, and I'm so shy I can't even make friends. . . . [Translated from Lakota by interviewer.]

Most of the newcomers seem to have a difficult time getting along with the experienced boarders and claim that the latter not only strip them of essentials like soap, paper, and underwear, but also take the treasured gifts of proud and encouraging relatives, wrist watches and transistor radios.

Some of the kids—especially the boarders—are really mean. All they want to do is steal—and they don't want to study. They'll steal your school work off you and they'll copy it. . . . Sometimes they'll break into our suitcase. Or if we have money in our pockets they'll take off our overalls and search our pockets and get our money. . . . So finally I just came home. If I could be a day scholar I think I'll stay in. But if they want me to board I don't want to go back. I think I'll just quit.

Interviews with the dropouts who asserted that school was "all right"—and that they had not wished to quit— suggest that many had been almost as wretched during their first weeks at high school as the bashful young men who quit because they "couldn't make friends." But they managed to find some friends and, with this peer support and protection, they were able to cope with and (probably) strike back at other boarders. In any case, the painful and degrading aspects of school became endurable. As one lad put it: "Once you *learn* to be a boarder, it's not so bad."

But for these young men, an essential part of having friends was "raising Cain"—that is, engaging in daring and defiant deeds forbidden by the school authorities. The spirit of these escapades is difficult to portray to members of a society where most people no longer seem capable of thinking about the modern equivalents of Tom Sawyer, Huckleberry Finn, or Kim, except as juvenile delinquents. We ourselves, burdened by sober professional interest in dropouts, at first found it hard to recognize that these able and engaging young men were taking pride and joy in doing exactly what the school authorities thought most reprehensible; and they were not confessing, but boasting, although their stunts had propelled them out of school.

For instance, this story from one bright lad of 15 who had run away from high school. Shortly after entering ninth grade he and his friends had appropriated a government car. (The usual pattern in such adventures is to drive off the reservation until the gas gives out.) For this offense (according to the respondent) they were restricted for the rest of the term—they were forbidden to leave the high school campus or attend any of the school recreational events, games, dances, or movies. (In effect, this meant doing nothing but going to class, performing work chores, and sitting in the dormitory.) Even then our respondent seems to have kept up with his class work and did not play hookey except in reading class:

It was after we stole that car Mrs. Bluger [pseudonym for reading teacher] would keep asking who stole the car in class. So I just quit going there. . . . One night we were the only ones up in the older boys' dorm. We said, "Hell with this noise. We're not going to be the only ones here." So we snuck out and went over to the dining hall. I pried this one window open about this far and then it started to crack, so I let it go. . . . We heard someone so we took off. It was show that night I think. [Motion picture was being shown in school auditorium.] . . . All the rest of the guys was sneaking in and getting something. So I said I was going to get my share too. We had a case of apples and a case of oranges. Then I think it was the night watchman was coming, so we run around and hid behind those steps. He shined that light on us. So I thought right then I was going to keep on going. That was around Christmas time. We walked back to Oglala [about 15 miles] and we were eating this stuff all the way back.

This young man implied that after this escapade he sim-

ply did not have the nerve to try to return to the high
school. He insisted, however, that he would like to try
another high school:

> I'd like to finish [high school] and get a good job some
> place. If I don't I'll probably just be a bum around here
> or something.

Roughly half the young Sioux who leave high school
very early claim they left because they were unable to con-
form to school regulations. What happens to the country
boys who remain? Do they "shape-up" and obey the regulations? Do they, even, come to "believe" in them? We
found that most of these older and more experienced
youths were, if anything, even *more* inclined to boast of
triumphs over the rules than the younger fellows who had
left. Indeed, all but one assured us that they were adept
at hookey, and food and car stealing, and that they had
frequent surreptitious beer parties and other outlaw en-
joyments. We do not know whether they (especially the
star athletes) actually disobey the school regulations as frequently and flagrantly as they claim. But there can be no
doubt that most Sioux young men above 12 wish to be regarded as hellions in school. For them, it would be un-
manly to have any other attitude.

An eleventh grader in good standing explained his
private technique for playing hookey and added proudly:
"They never caught me yet." A twelfth grader and first-
string basketball player told how he and some other students "stole" a jeep from the high school machine shop
and drove it all over town. When asked why, he patiently
explained: "To see if we can get away with it. It's for the
enjoyment . . . to see if we can take the car without getting
caught." Another senior told our male staff worker: "You
can always get out and booze it up."

The impulse to boast of the virile achievements of youth seems to maintain itself into middle and even into old age. Country Indians with college training zestfully told how they and a group of proctors had stolen large amounts of food from the high school kitchen and were never apprehended, or how they and their friends drank three fifths of whiskey in one night and did not pass out.

Clearly, the activities school administrators and teachers denounce as immature and delinquent are regarded as part of youthful daring, excitement, manly honor, and contests of skill and wits by the Sioux young men and many of their elders.

They are also, we suspect, an integral part of the world of competitive sports. "I like to play basketball" was one of the most frequent responses of young men to the question: "What do you like most about school?" Indeed, several ninth and tenth graders stated that the opportunity to play basketball was the main reason they kept going to school. One eighth grader who had run away several times stated:

When I was in the seventh grade I made the B team on the basketball squad. And I made the A team when I was in the eighth grade. So I stayed and finished school without running away anymore.

The unselfconscious devotion and ardor with which many of these young men participate in sports must be witnessed to be appreciated even mildly. They cannot communicate their joy and pride in words, though one 17-year-old member of the team that won the state championship tried, by telling how a team member wearing a war bonnet "led us onto the playing floor and this really gave them a cheer."

Unfortunately, we have seen little evidence that school administrators and teachers recognize the opportunity to use sports as a bridge to school.

By the eleventh and twelfth grades many country Indians have left the reservation or gone into the armed services, and it is not always easy to tell which are actual dropouts. However, we did reach some. Their reasons for dropping out varied. One pled boredom: "I was just sitting there doing anything to pass the time." Another said he didn't know what made him quit: "I just didn't fit in anymore. . . . I just wasn't like the other guys anymore." Another refused to attend a class in which he felt the teacher had insulted Indians. When the principal told him that he must attend this class or be "restricted," he left. Significantly, his best friend dropped out with him, even though he was on the way to becoming a first-class basketball player.

Different as they appear at first, these statements have a common undertone: They are the expressions not of immature delinquents, but of relatively mature young men who find the atmosphere of the high school stultifying and childish.

Any intense cross-cultural study is likely to reveal as many tragi-comic situations as social scientific insights. Thus, on the Pine Ridge reservation, a majority of the young men arrive at adolescence valuing *élan,* bravery, generosity, passion, and luck, and admiring outstanding talent in athletics, singing, and dancing. While capable of wider relations and reciprocities, they function at their social best as members of small groups of peers or relatives. Yet to obtain even modest employment in the greater society, they must graduate from high school. And in order to graduate from high school, they are told that they must develop exactly opposite qualities to those they possess: a respect for humdrum diligence and routine, for "discipline" (in the sense of not smoking in toilets, not cutting classes, and not getting drunk), and for government property. In addition, they are expected to compete scholastically on a highly privatized and individualistic level, while living in large dormitories, surrounded by strangers who make privacy of any type impossible.

If we were dealing with the schools of a generation or two ago, then the situation might be bettered by democratization—involving the Sioux parents in control of the schools. This system of local control was not perfect, but it worked pretty well. Today the problem is more complicated and tricky; educators have become professionalized, and educational systems have become complex bureaucracies, inextricably involved with universities, education associations, foundations, and federal crash programs. Even suburban middle class parents, some of whom are highly educated and sophisticated, find it difficult to cope with the bureaucratic barriers and mazes of the schools their children attend. It is difficult to see how Sioux parents could accomplish much unless, in some way, their own school system were kept artificially small and isolated and accessible to their understanding and control.

How does our study of the Sioux relate to the problems of city dropouts? A specific comparison of the Sioux dropouts with dropouts from the urban working class—Negroes, Puerto Ricans, or whites—would, no doubt, reveal many salient differences in cultural background and world view. Nevertheless, investigations so far undertaken suggest that the attitudes held by these peoples *toward education and the schools* are startlingly similar.

Both Sioux and working class parents wish their children to continue in school because they believe that graduating from high school is a guarantee of employment. Though some teachers would not believe it, many working class dropouts, like the Sioux dropouts, express a generally favorable attitude toward school, stating that teachers are generally fair and that the worst thing about dropping out of school is missing one's friends. Most important, many working class dropouts assert that they were pushed out of school and frequently add that the push was fairly direct. The Sioux boys put the matter more delicately, implying that the school authorities would not really welcome them back.

These similarities should not be seized on as evidence that all disprivileged children are alike and that they will respond as one to the single, ideal, educational policy. What it does mean is that the schools and their administrators are so monotonously alike that the boy brought up in a minority social or ethnic community can only look at and react to them in the same way. Despite their differences, they are all in much the same boat as they face the great monolith of middle-class society and its one-track education escalator.

An even more important—if often unrecognized—point is that not only does the school pose a dilemma for the working-class or Sioux, Negro, or Puerto Rican boy—he also poses one for the school. In many traditional or ethnic cultures boys are encouraged to be virile adolescents and become "real men." But our schools try to deprive youth of adolescence—and they demand that high school students behave like "mature people"—which, in our culture often seems to mean in a pretty dull, conformist fashion.

Those who submit and succeed in school can often fit into the bureaucratic requirements of employers, but they are also likely to lack independence of thought and creativity. The dropouts are failures—they have failed to become what the school demands. But the school has failed also—failed to offer what the boys from even the most "deprived" and "under-developed" peoples take as a matter of course

—the opportunity to become whole men.

S. M. Miller and Ira E. Harrison, studying working class youth, assert that individuals who do poorly in school are handicapped or disfavored for the remainder of their lives, because "the schools have become the occupational gatekeepers" and "the level of education affects the kind and level of job that can be attained." On the other hand, the investigations of Edgar Z. Friedenberg and Jules Henry suggest that the youths who perform creditably in high school according to the views of the authorities are disfavored in that they emerge from this experience as permanently crippled persons or human beings.

In a curious way our researches among the Sioux may be viewed as supporting both of these contentions, for they suggest that some young people leave high school because they are too vital and independent to submit to a dehumanizing situation.

May 1967

Renaissance and Repression: The Oklahoma Cherokee

ALBERT L. WAHRHAFTIG/ROBERT K. THOMAS

A week in eastern Oklahoma demonstrates to most outsiders that the Cherokee Indians are a populous and lively
community: Indians *par excellence.* Still, whites in eastern
Oklahoma unanimously declare the Cherokees to be a vanishing breed. Prominent whites say with pride, "we're all
a little bit Indian here." They maintain that real Cherokees
are about "bred out." Few Cherokees are left who can speak
their native tongue, whites insist, and fewer still are
learning their language. In twenty years, according to white
myth, the Cherokee language and with it the separate
and distinctive community that speaks it will fade into
memory.

Astonishingly, this pervasive social fiction disguises the
presence of one of the largest and most traditional tribes
of American Indians. Six rural counties in northeastern
Oklahoma contain more than fifty Cherokee settlements
with a population of more than 9,500. An additional 2,000
Cherokees live in Indian enclaves in towns and small cities.

Anthropologists visiting us in the field, men who thought their previous studies had taught them what a conservative tribe. is like, were astonished by Cherokees. Seldom had they seen people who speak so little English, who are so unshakably traditional in outlook.

How can native whites overlook this very identifiable Indian community? The answers, we believe, will give us not only an intriguing insight into the nature of Oklahoma society, but also some general conclusions about the position of other ethnic groups in American society.

This myth of Cherokee assimilation gives sanction to the social system of which Cherokees are a part, and to the position Cherokees have within that system. This image of the vanishing Cherokee in some ways is reminiscent both of the conservative Southern mythology which asserts that "our colored folk are a contented and carefree lot," and of the liberal Northern mythology, which asserts that "Negroes are just like whites except for the color of their skins." The fiction serves to keep Cherokees in place as a docile and exploitable minority population; it gives an official rationale to an existing, historic social system; and it implies that when the Indian Territory, the last Indian refuge, was dissolved, no Indian was betrayed, but all were absorbed into the mainstream.

The roots of modern eastern Oklahoma are in the rural South. Cherokees, and whites, came from the South; Cherokees from Georgia and Tennessee; and whites from Tennessee, Kentucky, Arkansas and southern Illinois.

In the years immediately preceding 1840, Cherokees, forced out of their sacred homelands in Georgia and Tennessee, marched over an infamous "Trail of Tears," and relocated in a new Cherokee Nation in what is now the state of Oklahoma. They created an international wonder: an autonomous Cherokee Nation with its own national constitution, legislature, judiciary, school system, publishing house, international bilingual newspaper, and many other trappings of a prosperous Republic. The Cherokees, who as a people accomplished all this, along with their neighbors, the Creeks, Choctaws, Chicasaws and Seminoles, who followed similar paths, were called the five civilized tribes.

Promising as the Cherokee Nation's future might have seemed, it was plagued by internal controversy from birth. Bitterness between the traditional Ross Party and the Treaty Party was intense. The Ross Party resisted demands for relocating from the South until its followers were finally corralled by the Army; the Treaty Party believed cooperation with the United States Government was the more prudent course for all Cherokees.

The sons and daughters of the Ross Party kept their ancient villages together. They reestablished these in the hollows and rough "Ozark" country of the Indian territory. Hewing new log cabins and planting new garden spots, they hoped to live unmolested by their opponents. They are today's "fullbloods," that is, traditional and Cherokee speaking Cherokees. On the other hand, descendants of the Treaty Party, who concentrated in the flat bottomlands and prairies they preferred for farming, are now assimilated and functionally white Americans, though fiercely proud of their Cherokee blood.

The Ross Party was the core of the Cherokee tribes. It was an institution which emerged from the experience of people who lived communally in settlements of kinsmen. The Treaty Party was a composite of individuals splintered from the tribal body. There were of course great differences in life style among nineteenth century Cherokee citizens. The Ross men, often well-educated, directed the Cherokee legislators from backwoods settlements. Treaty Party men were more often plantation owners, merchants, entrepreneurs, and professionals—conventional southern gentlemen. The overriding difference between the two factions, however, was between men who lived for their community and men who lived for themselves.

During the 1880's this difference came to be associated not with party but with blood. Geographically separated and ostracized by Ross men, members of the Treaty Party perforce married among the growing population of opportunistic whites who squatted on Indian land, defying U.S. and Cherokee law. The Treaty Party became known as the "mixed blood" faction of the tribe; the Ross Party as "full bloods." These terms imply that miscegenation caused a change of life style, a reversal of the historic events.

By 1907 when the Cherokee Nation was dissolved by Congressional fiat and the State of Oklahoma was created, the mixed bloods were already socially if not politically, part of the white population of the United States. The Ross Party settlements, now the whole of the functionally Cherokee population, are intact but surrounded by an assimilated population of mixed blood Cherokees integrated with white immigrants.

From the 1890s to 1920s, development of this area was astonishingly rapid. A flood of whites arrived. Land was populated by subsistence farmers, small town trade boomed, commercial farming expanded, railroads were built, timber exhausted, petroleum exploited and token industrialization established.

Already shorn of their nation, fullbloods were stunned and disadvantaged by the overnight expansion and growth. Change was rapid, the class system open. Future distinguished elders of small town society arrived as raggedy tots in the back of one-mule wagons. Not only was social mobility easy, few questions were asked about how the newly rich became rich. Incredible land swindles were commonplace. At the turn of the century, every square inch of eastern Oklahoma was alloted to Cherokees; by the 1930s little acreage remained in Indian possession.

The result of this explosive development was a remarkably stratified society, characterized by highly personal relationships, old time rural political machines, Protestant fundamentalism, reverence of free enterprise, and unscrupulous exploitation; in short, a system typical of the rural south.

Superficially, this society appears to be one with the most resourceful at the top, and the unworthy, who let opportunity slip by, at the bottom. In reality, however, the system consists of ranked ethnic groups, rather than classes. The successful old mixed-blood families, now functionally "white," whose self-identification as "Cherokee" is taken as a claim to the venerable status of "original settlers," dominate. Below them are the prosperous whites who "made something of themselves," and at the bottom, beneath the poor country whites, Cherokee "full bloods."

In primitive tribes, myth is a sacred explanation of the creation of the tribe and of its subsequent history. Myth specifies the holy design within which man was set to live. The fiction of Cherokee assimilation illustrates that modern man still uses myth, though differently. For in Oklahoma, the myth of Cherokee assimilation validates the social conditions men themselves have created, justifying the rightness and inevitability of what was done. As Oklahomans see it, the demise of the Cherokee as a people was tragic, albeit necessary. For only thus were individual Cherokees able to share in the American dream. The Oklahoman conceives of his society as an aggregate of individuals ranked by class, with unlimited opportunity for mobility regardless of individual ancestry. The high class position of the old Cherokee mixed-bloods signifies to the Oklahoman that the job of building Oklahoma was well done. The "responsible" Indians made it. The Cherokees, as a single historic people, died without heirs, and rightfully all those who settled on their estate now share in the distribution of its assets. For the culturally Indian individuals remaining, Oklahoma can only hope that they will do better in the future.

Even as the mythology serves to sanctify their high rank

position, it insulates whites from the recognition of the Cherokee as a viable but low ranked ethnic community with unique collective aims and interests. Where a real community exists, Oklahomans see only a residue of low status individuals. The myth, by altering perceptions, becomes self-perpetuating.

Paradoxically, the myth of Cherokee assimilation has also contributed to the survival of the Cherokee as a people. To the extent that Cherokees believed the myth, and many did, it was not only an explanation of how the tribe came into the present but a cohesive force. Since the end of a tribal movement led by Redbird Smith, a half century ago, in response to the final pressures for Oklahoma statehood, Cherokees have seemed inert, hardly a living people. Nevertheless, Cherokee communal life persisted, and is in a surprisingly healthy state. Cherokee settlements remain isolated, and if what goes on in them is not hidden, it is calculatedly inconspicuous. For the freedom from interference that it afforded, Cherokees willingly acceded to the notion that the Cherokees no longer exist.

In addition to sanctioning the form of Oklahoma society, the myth also gives credence to basic social and economic institutions. The economy of the area depends on Cherokees and country whites as an inexpensive and permanent labor market. Cherokees are expected to do low paying manual work without complaint. In 1963 Cherokee median per capita income, approximately $500, was less than half the per capita income of neighboring rural whites. In some areas, Cherokees live in virtual peonage; in others, straw bosses recruit Cherokee laborers for irregular work at low pay. Even though Cherokee communities are relatively hidden, Cherokee labor has become an indispensable part of the local economy. Apparently one would think that daily contact of white workers and bosses with these Cherokee laborers might expose the myth of the well-off assimilated Cherokee. On the contrary, the myth prevails because the humble occupations practiced by Cherokees are seen as evidence that Cherokee character is indeed that which the myth of assimilation predicts.

Imbedded in the Oklahoma concept of assimilation, is a glaring racism. Typical is the introductory page of a book published in 1938 entitled *A Political History of the Cherokee Nation,* written by Morris Wardell, a professor at the University of Oklahoma.

A selection: "Traders, soldiers, and treaty-makers came among the Cherokees to trade, compel and negotiate. Some of these visitors married Indian women and lived in the Indian villages the remainder of their days. Children born to such unions preferred the open and free life and here grew to manhood and womanhood, never going to the white settlements. The mixture of blood helped to produce strategy and cleverness which made formidable diplomats of many of the Indian leaders."

To white genes go the credit for Sequoyah's genius and John Ross's astuteness, whereas the remaining Cherokee genes contribute qualities that are endearing but less productive. Thus, in a history of the Cherokees published only six years ago, the author, an Oklahoman, says of modern "fullbloods": "They supplement their small income from farms and subsidies from the government with wage work or seasonal jobs in nearby towns or on farms belonging to white men. . . . Paid fair wages, this type of worker usually spends his money as quickly as he makes it on whisky, and on cars, washing machines, and other items that, uncared for, soon fall into necessitous disuse."

Oklahomans divide the contemporary Cherokees into two categories: those who are progressive and those who are not. The page just quoted continues, "this progressive type of Indian will not long remain in the background of the growing and thriving, and comparatively new, State of Oklahoma." That a viable Indian tribe exists is apparently inconceivable. Either Cherokees are worthy, responsible and assimilating, or they are the dregs; irresponsible, deculturated and racially inferior.

Through mythology, the exploitation of Cherokee labor is redefined into benevolent paternalism. Some patrons have Cherokees deliver their welfare checks to them, deduct from these housing and groceries. Afterwards the remainder is handed over to Cherokee tenants. Unknown to the welfare department, these same Cherokees receive stingy wages for working land and orchards belonging to the patron or to his kin. Patrons consider that they are providing employment and a steady paternal hand for unfortunate people who they contend could never manage themselves. The same ethic enables whites in good conscience to direct vestigal Cherokee tribal affairs; including the disbursement of well over two million dollars in funds left from a tribal land claim settlement.

It might seem odd that no one seeking to improve his position in the local establishment has ever tried to weaken these relationships. Why has no political figure taken cognizance of those thousands of Cherokee votes, and championed their cause? Instead politicians rely on the inefficient machinery of county patronage to collect Cherokee ballots. Unfortunately no one has yet dared, because fear binds the system. Older whites remember living in fear of a blood bath. The proposal to create Oklahoma meant a new state to whites; to Cherokees it meant the end of their own national existence. Their resistance to statehood was most desperate. Cherokees were a force to be contended with. They were feared as an ominously silent, chillingly mysterious people, unpredictable and violent. And Cherokees did organize into secret societies, much akin to the committees of twenty-five delegated in days past to murder collaborators who signed treaties. The reward of public office, politicians feel, does not justify the risk of rekindling that flame. To the extent that Oklahomans are aware of the numbers of Cherokees and the force they might generate, the myth of the assimilated Cherokee is a form of wishful thinking.

Finally, the myth protects the specific relationships of

rank and power which determine the stability of the present eastern Oklahoma social system. It does this in the following ways: By preventing recognition by whites and Indians alike of the Cherokees as a permanent community of people whose demands and aspirations must be taken seriously, it allows whites to direct the affairs of the region as they see fit.

By causing Cherokee aspirations to be discounted as romantic and irrelevant, it prevents the emergence of a competitive Cherokee leadership and discourages Cherokees from taking action as a community. For example, by 1904 Cherokees were given what was thought of as an opportunity to develop individualism and responsibility. The U.S. Government divided their communally owned land and each Indian was given his own piece. Thus the efforts of the present day Cherokee Four Mothers Society to piece together individual land holdings, reestablish communal title, and develop cooperative productive enterprises, is smilingly dismissed as an atavistic retreat to "clannishness."

By fostering the notion that Cherokees are an aggregate of disoriented individuals, it allows whites to plan for Cherokees, to control Cherokee resources, and to reinforce their own power by directing programs devoted to Cherokee advancement.

By denying that there is a Cherokee community with which a Cherokee middle class could identify and to which a Cherokee middle class could be responsive, it draws off educated Cherokees into "white" society and leaves an educationally impoverished pool of Cherokees to perpetuate the image of Cherokee incompetence.

The myth prevents scholars, Indian interest organizations, and the like from becoming overly curious about the area. If Cherokees are assimilated and prosperous, as the myth implies, there is neither a problem nor a culture to study. For 40 years no social scientist has completed a major study of any of the five civilized tribes. For 40 years the spread of information which might cast doubt on the myth itself has been successfully impeded.

In all, the myth stabilizes and disguises the Oklahoma social system.

The stability of a local social system, such as that of eastern Oklahoma, is heavily influenced by events in the larger society. The past decade of civil rights activity shook Oklahoma. Gradually, Oklahomans are becoming aware that their society is not as virtuous, homogeneous, attractive, and open as they may have supposed. And Oklahomans will now have to deal with the old agrarian social system of Cherokees, hillbillies, mixed-blood Cherokees, and a new urban elite grafted onto the old.

Left behind in the rush of workers to industry and of power to industrialized areas, the Ozark east of Oklahoma is a shell, depopulated, and controlled by newly dominant cities, Tulsa and Oklahoma City. The area, quaint enough to attract tourists, is far too rustic for sophisticated Oklahoma urbanites to take seriously. Local politicians offer weak leadership. Beginning to suspect that the local establishment is no longer all powerful, Cherokees have begun to assert themselves as a tribal community. The Cherokees conceive of themselves as a civilized nation, waiting for the dark days of the foreigners' suppression and exploitation to end. Oklahomans regard Cherokees as an aggregate of disadvantaged people still in the background of an integrated state, a definition which Cherokees do not share. In fact, the Cherokees are flirting with political office and have entered the courts with a hunting rights case. In launching a "Five County Northeast Oklahoma Cherokee Organization," they are gaining recognition as a legitimate community with rights, aspirations, resources and competence.

Consequently, the reappearance of assimilated Cherokees threatens the newly emergent regional power structure. Cherokees and the local establishment have begun jousting on a field of honor extending from county welfare offices (where the welfare-sponsored jobs of suspect members of the "Five County Organizations" are in jeopardy) to annual conventions of the National Congress of American Indians. Besides threatening an already shaky white power structure, the militant Cherokees are challenging the self esteem of the elderly and powerful "assimilated." Curiously, many white Oklahomans do not appear to be alarmed, but pleased, apparently, to relieve the tension that has developed between conflicting images of pretended assimilation and the reality of a workaday world.

The manner in which Oklahomans view their society is the manner in which American sociologists all too often view American society. Great emphasis is placed on class and on individual mobility. And, social description, in these terms, is seen very much as a product of the American ethos.

White Oklahomans consider themselves members of a class-stratified society in which any individual (Negroes excepted) has free access to any class. Descriptions of that system vary according to who is doing the describing. Generally, white Oklahomans conceive their society to be one in which the upper class is made up of prosperous whites and old Cherokee mixed-blood families, or their descendants; next in order is a layer of middle class whites and assimilated Cherokees; then, a lower class of poor, country whites, full-blood Cherokees and Negroes. Young liberals see a two-class system: A middle class of "decent" whites and Cherokees and socially unacceptable class of poor, country whites, Cherokees and Negroes.

This latter classification suggests that younger people perceive a much more closed system than their elders. Everyone is viewed as part of the same *community*—a word Oklahomans are fond of using. Presumably all groups of people have an equal share in the life of the community. Nationality, the word Oklahomans use to denote ethnic origin, is a principal clue to class position. As evidence of how open their society is, eastern Oklahomans point to Cherokees and poor, country whites (although not yet to Negroes, to whom the system is closed) who occupy respected positions. These are store owners, bureaucrats, and entrepreneurs; Babbitts of the 1960's, though born of traditional Cherokee parents. Always, however, these have been individuals who followed the only approved channel of mobility by scrupulously conforming to standards of behavior defined by those in control of the system.

The classic sociological studies on class in America, such as those by W. Lloyd Warner and Robert Lynd, are essentially static descriptions of the rank position of aggregates of individuals similar to the native Oklahoman's conception of his society. These studies reflect a peculiarly American bias. First, they examine the system that has formed rather than study how the system was formed. Americans are phenomenologists, more concerned with the things they have created than with the lengthy processes whereby these things have developed, more interested in ends than concerned with means.

Secondly, Americans do not stress ethnic considerations. In the American dream all individuals can "make it," regardless of nationality. For sociologists, class is a phenomenon in which individuals have social rank; ethnicity is treated as no more than an important clue in determining that rank. Thus, to be Irish was to be an outcast in nineteenth century Boston; not so today.

Thirdly, Americans, envisioning themselves as a nation of individualists, have assumed that social mobility for the most part rests on individual achievement. Immigrant groups are seen as having migrated into lower class positions in a relatively fixed class system through which individual immigrants rapidly became mobile. By contrast, Oklahoma's rapid entry into the formative American industrial economy caused a class-like structure to form on top of pre-existing ethnic communities.

A more balanced view shows that in the parts of the United States which industrialized earlier and more gradually, whole immigrant communities were successively imported into and butted one another through a social system which was in the process of formation and closure. The ways in which entire ethnic communities achieve mobility are overlooked.

Now it is becoming obvious that this mobility has slowed, even for those ethnic communities (like Poles) already "in the system." For communities which were brought into the system late (like Puerto Ricans) or at its territorial fringe (like Mexican-Americans in the Southwest) the situation is different.

Cherokees maintained technical independence as an autonomous nation until 1907, and in fact held America at arm's length until the 1890's. They provide an example of incorporation of an ethnic group into the industrial system in an area where no earlier group has paved the way. Thus, Cherokees are a "case type" which illustrated the modern dynamics of our system in pure form. Cherokees are now caught in our "historically mature" system of rank ethnic groups—a system which, for some, is rigid and closed, with little chance for individual and less for communal mobility. The total rank-structure of eastern Oklahoma is cemented by the mythology Americans use to obscure and rationalize their privileged position in a closed system.

In their conception of class, American sociologists are often as wedded to myth as are Oklahomans, and the resulting large areas of American social science they have created obediently subscribe to official fictions within the American world view.

Now, successive summers of violence have exploded some of the folk and scientific mythology shrouding the structure of our nation. The *Report of the National Advisory Commission on Civil Disorders* declares: "What white

Americans have never fully understood—but what the Negro can never forget—is that white society is deeply implicated in the ghetto. White institutions created it, white institutions maintain it, and white society condones it." Yet throughout this unusually clear report the phenomenon of white racism is barely alluded to, as though it were an "attitude" born by an uninformed populace and unrelated to the core of our national social system. That system, as we see it in operation in Oklahoma, beneath its mythology of assimilation, consists of a structure of ranked ethnic groups, euphemistically called "classes" by American sociologists; a structure which is growing more stable and more rigid. This kind of structure is general in America and, of course, implied in the above quote from the Kerner report. In Oklahoma such a system of relationships has enabled aggressive entrepreneurs to harness and utilize the resources of ethnic communities which are frozen into a low ranked position by the dominant community's control over channels of mobility and by the insistence that the whole complex represents one single community differentiated only by personal capability. Thus, essentially "racist" perceptions and relationships are the "motor" driving the system and are embedded in the very day-to-day relationships of middle class Oklahoma.

February 1969

FURTHER READING SUGGESTED BY THE AUTHORS:

And Still the Waters Run by Angie Debo (Princeton University Press, 1940) is a historian's meticulous account of the techniques through which the Five Civilized Tribes were stripped of their resources at the beginning of this century.
The New Indians by Stan Steiner (Harper and Row, 1968). Chapter one presents a portrait of spokesmen for the present community of traditional Cherokee Indians and an account of their efforts to buck the Oklahoma "establishment."

White Rites
and Indian Rights

ANTHONY D. FISHER

The lyrics of a song in the top ten last summer put the matter unequivocally. "Education's the thing," wails the lead singer of a black group called The Winstons, "if you want to compete. Without it, life just ain't very sweet." Almost everyone in North America, I suspect, would say "Amen" to that. The belief in increasing educational opportunities as the avenue to social progress has become an article of faith, and "going to school" an assurance of secular salvation akin to "good works" and "saving grace" in other times and other religions.

That for many sectors of North American society this belief flies in the face of observable facts should surprise no one. Yet it is a fact that the propitiation of the gods of learning simply isn't working for vast numbers of Americans and Canadians, especially the poor, the black and the Indian. Indeed, for those with whom I am most concerned in this essay, the Indian people of Canada, it can be demonstrated that education has been very nearly a total disaster.

Despite a considerable expansion of the number of schools and in the number of years of schooling available to Canadian Indian children, the unemployment rate among them has increased. Between the years 1959-60 and 1962-63, the welfare costs among Alberta's Indian population jumped from $294,625 to $683,080, and a sizeable portion of the latter figure went to unemployed but "educated" Indians. The incidence of unemployment among Indians with education is even more graphically illustrated by comparing the average unemployment of the total Indian population (43 percent) to that of Alberta Indian students who terminated their education in 1964-65 (64 percent).

While these figures clearly indicate that the Canadian Indian fails to use whatever education he receives once his schooling is over, other studies show that he also fails to take advantage of the schooling available to him. For example, in 1965 a study was made of junior high school dropouts at the Blackfoot Indian Reserve, Gleichen-Cluny, Alberta. It was determined that 86 of 168 students, or 51 percent, had dropped out of school in the years since 1961 and of these dropouts, 95 percent left school before they had completed grade nine. Something quite obviously happened to these children between grades five and nine.

Numerous hypotheses have been advanced to explain the phenomenon of the school dropout by persons of lower socioeconomic class; however none has been wholly satisfactory. This essay is an attempt to account for the phenomenon in a more fruitful manner, by redefining the dropout situation, and by applying this definition to the specific case of dropouts among Canadian Indians.

It will be useful to list some hypotheses used to explain dropping out, not because they are the most important or the most misleading, but because they illustrate the direction of concern among various students of education. Seymour Rubenfeld, in his 1965 study, *Family of Outcasts,* offers the hypothesis that the dropout as well as the juvenile delinquent gets that way because of an incomplete socialization that results in a self-discontent which is then externalized and "lived out" through deviant behavior, some of which is in relation to the school.

Lucius F. Cervantes' *The Dropout: Causes and Cures* presents the dropout as suffering from the failure of his primary group, his family. The result of this failure is the inability to achieve success in primary interpersonal relationships, which produces personality disorganization. This causes an end to interpersonal communication and makes personal satisfaction unattainable. For these reasons the individual leaves school.

Richard Cloward and Lloyd Ohlin, in the immensely influential *Delinquency and Opportunity,* focus on what might be called "objective status discontent." This implies that the deviant or delinquent individual is alienated from his environment and the legitimate means to success in that environment, (e.g. "education") because these institutions are, quite objectively, alienating. Because of this alienation, however, the individual turns to illegitimate means to nurture success. Another author utilizing the theme of alienation is John F. Bryde, who sees the Indian student of South Dakota as literally being outside of and between both Indian and white-man cultures. As such, he is alienated from both the goals of education and his Indian identity, which leads to his scholastic failure and "dropping out."

Finally, Murray and Rosalie Wax's study of the same Sioux Indian students that Bryde discussed, indicates that one of the major causes of dropping out is what can be called "institutional intolerance." The Waxes argue that the school situation at Pine Ridge, South Dakota, is characterized by a lack of communication between the school functionaries and those they serve. There is "social distance" between students and teachers and considerable individual isolation, even within the same school.

These explanations appear to be suitable for the particular cases they describe. Almost all of them, however, concentrate upon one variable, the student or ex-student. They fail to consider the institutional and cultural variable, the school. It is the latter that I shall focus on in this essay.

In Euro-Canadian society the school is a "primary institution," in the sense that it is basic and widespread. All Euro-Canadian children are expected to attend school for extensive periods of time and to profit from the experience. It is, in fact and in theory, the major socialization device of the industrialized, urbanized segment of the Canadian population. As such it consumes a tremendous amount of time, substantial amounts of money and a great deal of energy.

In this paper, then, I define "the school," all formal education from kindergarten to grade twelve or thirteen, as a rite of passage, or rather a series of rites signifying separation from, transition through and incorporation into culturally recognized statuses and roles. Within the larger chronological rite there are also numerous other rites and ceremonials indicating partial transitions and new role relationships.

This redefinition of the school as a rite of passage is likely to provoke some disagreement. Anthropologists and laymen alike choose to think of ritual and rites of passage as essentially magico-religious activities, and of schools as being only partially or minimally engaged in this type of activity. This is not altogether so. Not all ritual must be magico-religious, nor are schools as institutions, or what goes on in schools, completely free from magico-religious significance. It is quite difficult to categorize ritual activity clearly as to religious content. Further, ritual activity ranges from the purely magical and religious through the pseudo-rational to rational routine, albeit it is up to the observer to ascertain its rationality. Clearly, in any case, there are numerous calendrical and other rites and ceremonies in the public school that signify changes in the student's social life. Thus, the whole educational structure can be envisioned as a long-term ritual marking various changes in the social lives of the individuals. It is difficult for an outside observer to assess their magico-religious or secular content.

Nevertheless, it would be very hard to argue that the majority of Canadian students, parents and teachers see "education" in a wholly rational light. In a recent study, a noted American educator pointed out that despite scientific knowledge to the contrary the vast majority of public school classrooms in the United States operate on the two-thirds theory (*Trans*-action, 1967): two-thirds of the time someone is talking, two-thirds of the time it is the teacher who is talking, two-thirds of the time the teacher is talking she is lecturing or commenting upon the behavior of children in the classroom. If this is the case in the United States, then Canadian schools, generally, operate on the three-quarters theory, and schools catering to Indians operate on the seven-eighths theory. The involvement of the school in teaching moral-ethical behavior, the continuing belief in "disciplining the mind" through rigid curricula and repetitive testing, the various rites of prayer and of patriotism, indeed, the whole defensive ethos of the school point to the pseudorational nature of the school.

More succinctly, one can look at "the school" as a series of "ideological rituals," using "ideological" here in Mannheim's sense, as a means to protect and perfect the existing social system, in contrast to the "utopian" striving for revolutionary change. In this sense the public school in North America is indeed an ideological rite of passage. Educators have long thought the institution of the public school as the common ground that allows immigrant and indigenous groups the wherewithal for intelligent self-government, common mores and economic perfection and advancement within the ideological system of North American "democratic" society.

There is little doubt that the characteristic form of North American public education is typical of North American society. It exemplifies and reflects the values of that society, and prepares students for urban, industrialized middle-class society. Finally the whole ritual culminates in a pseudoreligious ceremonial known as "Convocation" or "Commencement" in which it tells the ex-student, "Now do it." Those who "can do it" have been certified for that society. From kindergarten or grade one when the child learns who his "helpers" in the school and neighborhood are, to grade twelve or thirteen when each student is ranked and evaluated on the formalized "external" or Departmental examinations, he passes through a multitude of statuses and plays many roles. The result of the whole process is the development of a particular sort of individual, that is if the process is successful.

But, what would happen if we were to take this ceremonial system out of its context, North American middle-class society, and place it in a wholly or partly alien context such as an Indian reserve? The answer is that unless there were community support for it, it would fail. Let me stress this point. It would be the rite of passage, the rituals recognized and enjoined by middle-class society that would fail; *not the Indian student.*

Since 1944 there has been little doubt among scholars that students of North American Indian ancestry have intelligence adequate for most activities, exclusive of school. Robert Havighurst's well-known 1957 article demonstrates that Indian children perform " . . . about as well . . . " as white children on performance tests of intelligence. More recently, in Charles Ray, Joan Ryan, and Seymour Parker's 1962 study of Alaskan secondary-school dropouts, the authors state:

> The conclusion to be derived from the data is that intelligence *per se* cannot be considerd a major contributing factor to dropouts and that achievement levels are not markedly different.

As this essay is focused primarily on dropouts with Eskimo, Aleut, or Tlingit ethnic backgrounds as contrasted with white children, it appears to indicate that the cause of dropout is elsewhere than intelligence. But where are we to find it?

California Achievement Test scores in Alberta and South Dakota among Plains Cree, Blackfoot and Sioux Indians indicate that the young Indian starts out *ahead* of his white peers, but then gradually tails off in achievement. Fourth-grade Indians who had averaged 4.3 on achievement tests while their white counterparts scored only 4.1, had by the eighth grade been surpassed by the white students who achieved an 8.1 average while Indian students had one of 7.7. Test scores consistently decline between grades five and seven. Furthermore, a parallel phenomenon in retardation of grade placement in relationship to age has been indicated in a study of Kwakiutl Indians on Gilford Island, British Columbia. The number of students at the expected grade-level decreased sharply from 4 at grade one to 1 by grade five and 0 by grade six. At the same time, the number of students *below* the expected grade-level increased from 2 at grade one to 4 at grade five. Similar studies done by the Waxes on South Dakota Sioux also reveal that between the fifth and seventh grade the number of students of appropriate grade-age decreases. Thus, where the majority of fifth-grade students are in the 10- to 11-year category, the majority of sixth-grade students are in the 12- to 13-year range. From these patterns of slumping achievement-test scores and increasing age-grade level retardation, it appears that some sort of difficulty arises in the relationship between "the school" and the pre-pubescent/pubescent Indian. Admittedly, some Indian students drop out later than others but it would appear that in most cases of prolonged schooling it is the enforcement of the School Act that made the difference. The Blackfoot and Blood Indians of southern Alberta, for example, are under considerable compulsion to stay in school. If they do not "fit" the existing academic program, they are enrolled in "pre-employment" courses or in special programs such as "upgrading." It is therefore quite difficult for these students to leave school. The younger student often "solves" this problem by becoming a "trouble-maker" in school (sassing teachers, being truant, refusing to work, etc.) or by becoming "delinquent" outside school (drinking and sexual escapades, fighting and theft). Of these Blackfoot "early dropouts," ages thirteen to sixteen (which is the school-leaving age) 75 percent of the fifteen-year-olds and 70 percent of the sixteen-year-olds were considered "delinquent." Among the older students, ages seventeen, eighteen and nineteen, the amount of delinquent behavior was radically reduced. Apparently, then, when a Blackfoot student passes the school-leaving age, he can choose to stay or to go, and he generally chooses to go.

Another difference leading to local variation in the school-leaving age may be the attitudes of Indians about what is appropriate for them in the school. What the Indian expects to get out of school, what it means to him and what he believes himself to be are really the critical issues. Even though the specific answers to these questions may vary with different tribes, the result of these answers is the same: early dropout and unused education.

Indian expectations of school are conditioned by what the young Indian learns in the environment of his home community. Because what he learns at home often differs widely from what he learns at school, the Indian student is frequently forced to separate the two learning experiences. George Spindler once heard a "successful" Blood Indian say:

I have to think about some things in my own language and some things in English. Well, for instance, if I think about horses, or about the Sun Dance, or about my brother-in-law, I have to think in my own language. If I think about buying a pickup truck or selling some beef or my son's grades in school I have to think in English.

The languages of Blackfoot and English are kept entirely apart; the former is for thinking about basic cultural elements, while the latter is used for school work. The Indian student grows up in a particular society with its own particular role transitions and in the presence of or absence of appropriate ritual recognition of these changes. Since the expectations about ritual and about role transitions held by any society and recognized as legitimate for that society are peculiar to that society, and to part-societies, at any time the school, as a rite of passage, may become inappropriate to members of a particular society that differs from North American middle-class society. This is what seems to happen to the Indian student.

Young Blood Indians have certain very specific ideas about what they are and what they are going to be. Among a stratified sample of forty young Bloods the most popular choices of a career or vocation were as follows: ranching, automechanic, carpenter, bronc rider, haying and farming. All of these occupations can be learned and practiced right on the Blood Reserve. They chose these occupations for two important reasons: knowledge and experience or, in other words, experiential knowledge that they already held. Among the Blackfoot dropouts and "stay-ins" a very similar pattern emerged. They, too, chose occupations that were familiar to them, even if they pertained little to their academic life. And this pattern emerges elsewhere in only slightly different form.

In Harry Wolcott's "Blackfish Village" Kwakiutl study he mentions in passing the response by students to the essay topic, "What I Would Like to Be Doing Ten Years from Now." Almost all the students thought they would be in and around their village. Two of the older girls guessed they would be married and in the village. Farther north, in Alaska, the Ray, Ryan and Parker study notes that the three primary reasons given for dropping out of secondary school are "needed at home," "marriage" and "wanted to work." Of the secondary reasons, to help at "home," "marriage" and "homesick" were most important. These reasons appear to indicate that the Alaskan dropout was opting out of formal education to return home to what he or she knows. As the authors indicate, "The majority of dropouts saw little relationship between what they were learning in school and jobs that were available to them."

Turning inland from British Columbia and Alaska we note the same phenomenon among the Metis of the Lac La Biche area (Kikino, Owl River, Mission), among the Blackfoot dropouts of Gleichen and Cluny and among the young Blood of southwestern Alberta. In each case the

Indian student on the one hand expects to be doing what is now done in the context of his community, and on the other hand sees only a vague, if any, correlation between the demands of formal education in the context of the school and that which he expects to do.

A final point in this regard is made in the Waxes' study of the Pine Ridge Sioux. They state that education and being a good Sioux Indian are two separate processes, if becoming a good Indian is a process at all. They say that the full-bloods think that:

. . . education harms no one, but on the other hand it has almost nothing to do with being a good person. . . . [They] do not seem to be aware that their offspring are regarded as unsocialized, amoral or backward by their teachers. That a child could be educated to the point where he would become critical of his kin or attempt to disassociate himself from them is still beyond their comprehension.

In conclusion, these studies show that the expanded educational opportunities for Canadian Indians are not really opportunities at all. For what the school offers is an irrelevant set of values and training. Moreover, the school often comes into direct conflict with certain moral and cultural values of the student. Thus, it is the educational system that fails the student and not the student who fails the system. In trying to be a good and successful Indian, the Indian student must often be a bad and unsuccessful student.

November 1969

Seminole Girl

MERWYN S. GABARINO

One hundred and thirty miles of circuitous road and 250 years of history separate the city of Miami from the four federal reservations that lock the Seminole Indians into the Florida swamplands, known as Big Cypress Swamp. A new road is under construction that will trim in half the traveling distance between the city and the reservations scattered along the present winding U.S. Highway 41 or Tamiami Trail as it is called by the Indians. But the new road will only draw the two communities closer on the speedometer; it will not alter the vastly different lifeways it links; it may only make more apparent the historical inequities that brought the two areas into existence.

The Seminoles are harsh examples of what happened to American Indians caught in the expansion process that saw the United States swell from a federation of 13 colonies to a nation blanketing more than half a continent. The peoples who came to be known as "Seminole," which

69

means "wild" or "undomesticated," were Indians who fled south from the guns and plows of the whites. Some were Yamassee who were driven from the Carolinas in 1715. Others were Hitchiti-speaking Oconee who moved down the Apalachicola River to settle in Spanish-held Florida. These two groups were joined by others escaping soldiers or settlers or other Indians demanding their lands.

The loose confederation of Seminoles was tripled by a large influx of Creeks after the Creek War of 1813–14. Although the Creeks were linguistically related to the Hitchiti, the primary factor uniting the diverse groups was the hatred and fear they felt toward their common foe, the young United States. But this common bond was enough to regroup the broken political units into a single body that absorbed not only Indians, but renegade whites and Negroes escaping slavery.

In 1817–18, the United States sent Andrew Jackson to Florida, ostensibly to recover runaway slaves. This resulted in the First Seminole War, one of the three Seminole Wars that were among the bloodiest ever fought by American forces against Indians. The war also led to the annexation of Florida by the U.S. in 1821 because Spain was in no position to fight for it.

At the time of annexation, the Indians held extensive farm and pasture lands that the Spaniards had not wanted for themselves. American settlers, however, wanted them very much. Insatiable, they forced the Seminoles ever southward, until finally they demanded that the Indians relocate to the area of the Louisiana Purchase which is now Oklahoma. Some Indians went westward, but a number under the leadership of Osceola fought bitterly. When Osceola was captured under a flag of truce, some of his warriors fled into the Everglades where they could not be flushed out. To this day they haven't recognized the treaty that drove their fellow tribesmen to the West.

In 1911, Florida reservation land was set aside by an executive order. The Seminoles, however, were not pressured at that time into moving on to the federal territory. South Florida was a real wilderness; Miami was little more than a town, and lavish coastal resorts were unforeseen. Literally no one but the alligators, snakes, birds and the Indians wanted the land they lived on. The climate is one of wet summers and dry winters, and the area is often struck by hurricanes from the Caribbean. Annual rainfall is in excess of 60 inches and without drainage, the prairie is almost always under water. Brush fires in the dry season destroy valuable hardwood trees on the hummocks which are the low-lying hills undulating through the swampland. Fire also destroys the highly flammable drained peat and for the same reason, there is an absence of pines in many areas suitable for their growth. Elsewhere however, there are moderately to heavily wooded places, and sometimes great flocks of white egrets alight in the branches of the trees, looking like puffs of white blossoms. Except for the hummocks, the horizon is flat, a vista of sky and water, broken only by the occasional wooded clumps.

Most inhabitants of this waste and water live on elevated platforms under thatched roofs held in place by poles. Unemployment is an ever-present problem helped somewhat by seasonal agricultural work or by crafts such as the gaily colored garments, dolls, basketry and carvings made for the tourists who are now visiting their homeland on a year 'round basis. Lands are leased to commercial vegetable farmers and deer can still be hunted. So subsistence living is still possible for the "wild" Seminoles.

Somewhere along the Tamiami Trail, Nellie Greene—a pseudonym of course—was born a Seminole, raised in a chickee, and learned the ways of her people. Her father was a frog hunter and could neither read nor write; her mother was a good Seminole mother who later had troubles with tuberculosis and drinking. No one Nellie knew had much more education than her father and mother. Yet, despite the ignorance and illiteracy on the reservation, Nellie Greene wanted and was encouraged to get a good. education. As it does for most Indians in the United States, this meant leaving her "backward" people, mixing with whites who at best patronized her.

I first met Nellie Greene when she had graduated from college and was living in an apartment in Miami where she worked as a bank clerk. I knew her background from having spent three summers in the middle sixties, thanks to the National Science Foundation, on the Seminole reservations of Florida. In September of 1966 Nellie wrote me that she had been offered a job as manager in the grocery store back on the reservation. If she didn't take it, a white person would, for she was the only native with the necessary knowledge of bookkeeping. She had accepted the job, she said, but since she had once told me (in Miami) that she could never give up the kind of life she had grown accustomed to there, I was curious to find out why she had returned to the reservation.

She herself said that she took the job to help her people, but she added that it had not been an easy decision; in fact it had been quite a struggle. I could have guessed that this was so; many Indian tribes that offer educational grants to their younger members do so only with the stipulation that the recipients later return to the reservation. The stipulation is a measure of the difficulty in getting

their educated members to come back to the tribe. In any
event, I wanted to hear Nellie Greene tell her own story.
I went to see her, and this is what she told me.

Nellie Greene's Story

I was born in a Miami hospital on February 6, 1943. At
that time my parents were living on the (Tamiami) Trail,
and my daddy was making his living frog hunting. He
owned an air boat and everything that goes along with
frog hunting. It was during the war, and at that time I
guess it was hard to get gas. When it was time for me to
be born, my father had to borrow gas from a farmer to get
to Miami. But the tail light was broken, so my father took
a flashlight and put a red cloth over it and tied it on to the
truck and went to the hospital. My daddy often told me
about that.

I had an older sister and an older brother. We lived in
a chickee until 1961 when my daddy bought a CBS (a
cement block structure, "hurricane proof" according to
state standards) at Big Cypress, and we moved into it.
When I was little, my daddy had to be out in the Everglades a lot, so he would take all of us out to a hummock,
and we would make camp there and stay there while he
went off to hunt for frogs. When he got back, he'd take the
frog legs into the hotels and sell them. Then he would
bring back something for each of us. When he would ask
us what we wanted, I always asked for chocolate candy.

About all I remember of the Everglades is that it was a
custom when you got up to take a bath or go swimming
early in the morning. My mother says they always had to
chase me because I didn't like to get wet in winter when
it was cold. We were there four or five years, and then we
moved near the Agency at Dania (renamed Hollywood in

1966). I had never been to school until then. We were taught at home, the traditional things: to share with each other and with children of other families, to eat after the others—father and grandfather first, then mothers and kids. But lots of times us kids would climb up on our father's knees while they were eating. They didn't say anything, and they'd give us something. It just wasn't the custom for families to eat the way we do today, everybody sitting together around the table.

Folktales, too, we learned; they were like education for us, you know. The stories told about someone doing something bad, and then something bad happened to him. That was the way of teaching right and wrong.

When we were growing up we broke away from some family customs. My parents spanked us, for instance, not my mother's brother, who would have been the right person to punish his sister's children—one of the old ways. But they were not close to my mother's family because my daddy was a frog hunter, and we wandered around with him. My parents were chosen for each other by their families. I guess they learned to love each other in some ways, but I have heard my mother say that it is not the same kind of love she would have had if she had chosen her own husband. It was respect, and that was the custom of the Indians.

Most parents here show so little affection. Even if they love their kids, maybe they don't think they should show love. I know a lot of parents who really care, but they don't tell their kids how they feel. We always knew how our parents felt about us. They showed us affection. Sometimes I hear kids say, "My mother doesn't care whether I go to school or not." These kids have seen how others get care from their parents, like the white children at school. And that kind of concern doesn't show up here. A lot of parents don't even think of telling their children that they want them to succeed. They don't communicate with their children. You never see an Indian mother here kiss and hug children going to school. But white parents do that, and when Indian children see this in town or on TV, it makes them think that Indian parents just don't care. Kids are just left to go to school or not as they wish. Often the mothers have already left to work in the fields before the school bus comes. So no one sees whether children even go to school.

I felt loved. My parents never neglected us. We have never gone without food or clothes or a home. I have always adored my mother. She has made her mistakes, but I still feel the same about her as when I was a child.

We moved to Big Cypress around 1951 or 1952. I had been in first grade at Dania. I remember I didn't understand English at all when I started first grade. I learned it then. We moved around between Big Cypress and Dania, visiting, or because my father was doing odd jobs here and there.

Both my parents wanted me to go to school because they had wanted to go to school when they were kids. I can remember my mother telling me that she and her sister wanted to go to school. But the clan elders—their uncles— wouldn't let them. The uncles said they would whip the two girls if they went.

One of my father's greatest desires was to go to school when he was a boy. He said that he used to sneak papers and pencils into the camp so that he could write the things he saw on the cardboard boxes that the groceries came in, and figures and words on canned goods. He thought he would learn to read and write by copying these things. My daddy adds columns of figures from left to right, and he subtracts the same way. His answers will be correct, but I don't know how. Almost everything he knows he learned on his own. He can understand English, but he stutters when he talks. He has a difficult time finding the right word when he speaks English, but he understands it.

When my parents said no, they meant no. That was important to me. They could be counted on. The other thing that was important in my childhood schooling was that my daddy always looked at my report card when I brought it home from school. He didn't really know what it meant, and he couldn't read, but he always looked at my report card and made me feel that he cared how I did in school. Other parents didn't do this. In fact, most of the kids never showed their parents their report cards. But my daddy made me feel that it was important to him. I told him what the marks stood for. It was rewarding for me because he took the time.

Public school was hard compared to what I'd had before, day school on the reservation and a year at Sequoyah Government School. I almost flunked eighth grade at the public school, and it was a miracle that I passed. I just didn't know a lot of things, mathematics and stuff. I survived it somehow. I don't know how, but I did. The man who was head of the department of education at the Agency was the only person outside of my family who helped me and encouraged me to get an education. He understood and really helped me with many things I didn't know about. For a long time the white public school for the Big Cypress area would not let Indian children attend. A boy and I were the first Big Cypress Indians to graduate from that school. He is now in the armed forces.

After I graduated from high school I went to business college, because in high school I didn't take courses that would prepare me for the university. I realized that there was nothing for me to do. I had no training. All I could do was go back to the reservation. I thought maybe I'd go to Haskell Institute, but my mother was in a TB hospital, and I didn't want to go too far away. I did want to go on to school and find some job and work. So the director of education said maybe he could work something out for me so I could go to school down here. I thought bookkeeping would be good because I had had that in high school and loved it. So I enrolled in the business college, but my English was so bad that I had an awful time. I had to take three extra months of English courses. But that helped me. I never did understand why my English was so bad—whether it was my fault or the English I had in high school. I thought I got by in high school; they never told me that my English was so inferior, but it was not good enough for college. It was *terrible* having to attend special classes.

At college the hardest thing was not loneliness but schoolwork itself. I had a roommate from Brighton (one of the three reservations), so I had someone to talk to. The landlady was awfully suspicious at first. We were Indians, you know. She would go through our apartment, and if we hadn't done the dishes, she washed them. We didn't like that. But then she learned to trust us.

College was so fast for me. Everyone knew so much more. It was as though I had never been to school before. As soon as I got home, I started studying. I read assignments both before and after the lectures. I read them before so I could understand what the professor was saying, and I read them again afterwards because he talked so fast. I was never sure I understood.

In college they dressed differently from high school, and I didn't know anything about that. I learned how to dress. For the first six weeks, though, I never went anywhere. I stayed home and studied. It was hard—real hard.

(I can imagine what a real university would be like.) And it was so different. If you didn't turn in your work, that was just your tough luck. No one kept at me the way they did in high school. They didn't say, "OK, I'll give you another week."

Gradually I started making friends. I guess some of them thought I was different. One boy asked me what part of India I was from. He didn't even know there were Indians in Florida. I said, "I'm an American." Things like that are kind of hard. I couldn't see my family often, but in a way that was helpful because I had to learn to adjust to my new environment. Nobody could help me but myself.

Well, I graduated and went down to the bank. The president of the bank had called the agency and said he would like to employ a qualified Indian girl. So I went down there and they gave me a test, and I was interviewed. And then they told me to come in the following Monday. That's how I went to work. I finished college May 29, and I went to work June 1. I worked there for three years.

In the fall of 1966, my father and the president of the Tribal Board asked me to come back to Big Cypress to manage a new economic enterprise there. It seemed like a dream come true, because I could not go back to live at Big Cypress without a job there. But it was not an easy decision. I liked my bank work. You might say I had fallen in love with banking. But all my life I had wanted to do something to help my people, and I could do that only by leaving my bank job in Miami. Being the person I am, I had to go back. I would have felt guilty if I had a chance to help and I didn't. But I told my daddy that I couldn't give him an answer right away, and I knew he was upset because he had expected me to jump at the chance to come back. He did understand though, that I had to think about it. He knew when I went to live off the reservation that I had had a pretty hard time, getting used to a job, getting used to people. He knew I had accomplished a lot, and it wasn't easy for me to give it up. But that's how I felt. I had to think. At one time it seemed to me that I could never go back to reservation life.

But then really, through it all, I always wished there was something, even the smallest thing, that I could do for my people. Maybe I'm helping now. But I can see that I may get tired of it in a year, or even less. But right now I'm glad to help build up the store. If it didn't work out, if the store failed, and I thought I hadn't even tried, I would really feel bad. The basic thing about my feeling is that my brothers and sisters and nieces and nephews can build later on in the future only through the foundation their parents and I build. Maybe Indian parents don't always show their affection, but they have taught us that, even though we have a problem, we are still supposed to help one another. And that is what I am trying to do. Even when we were kids, if we had something and other kids didn't, we must share what we had with the others. Kids grow up the way their parents train them.

By the age of nine, girls were expected to take complete care of younger children. I too had to take care of my little brother and sister. I grew up fast. That's just what parents expected. Now teen-agers don't want to do that, so they get angry and take off. Headstart and nurseries help the working mothers because older children don't tend the little ones any more. The old ways are changing, and I hope to help some of the people, particularly girls about my age, change to something good.

There are people on the reservation who don't seem to like me. Maybe they are jealous, but I don't know why. I know they resent me somehow. When I used to come in from school or from work back to the reservation, I could tell some people felt like this. I don't think that I have ever, ever, even in the smallest way, tried to prove myself better or more knowing than other people. I have two close friends here, so I don't feel too lonely; but other people my age do not make friends with me. I miss my sister, and I miss my roommate from Miami. My two friends here are good friends. I can tell them anything I want. I can talk to them. That's important, that I can talk to them. That's what I look for in a friend, not their education, but for enjoyment of the same things, and understanding. But there are only two of them. I have not been able to find other friends.

The old people think I know everything because I've been to school. They think it is a good thing for us to go to school. But the old people don't have the kind of experience which allows them to understand our problems. They think that it is easy somehow to come back here. They think there is nothing else. They do not understand that there are things I miss on the outside. They do not understand enough to be friends. They are kind, and they are glad that I am educated, but they do not understand my problems. They do not understand loneliness.

It was hard for me to get used again to the way people talk. They have nothing interesting to talk about. They are satisfied to have a TV or radio, but they don't know anything about good books or good movies or the news. There is almost no one I have to talk to about things like that. Here people don't know what discussion is. That's something I found really hard. They gossip: they talk about people, not ideas.

And it was hard getting used to what people think about time. You know, when you live in the city and work, everything is according to time. You race yourself to death, really. But I got used to that and put myself on a schedule. But here, when you want something done, people take their time. They don't come to work when they should, and I just don't want to push them. I would expect it of the older people, but the younger generation should realize how important time is. When you go to school, you just eat and study and go to school, and not worry too much about time; but on a job, you must keep pace. You are being paid for a certain performance. If you do not do what you are supposed to, you do not get paid. But how do I get that across to my people?

I was lonely when I first came back here. I was ready to pack up and go back to Miami. People hardly talked to me —just a few words. I don't know why. I've known these people all my life. I don't know why they didn't know me after just three years. I couldn't carry on a conversation with anyone except my own family. I was working all day at the store, and then I had nothing to do but clean the house, or go fishing alone, or with someone from my family.

Coming back to the reservation to live did not seem to be physically hard. At first I lived in a house with a girl friend because I did not want to stay with my family. I wanted to be sure of my independence. I think this hurt my father. But later, when more of my friend's family moved back to the reservation, I decided it was too crowded with her and went back to live in my old home with my father and family. My father's CBS is clean and comfortable. It is as nice as an apartment in Miami.

My idea was that, being raised on the reservation and knowing the problems here, I could hope that the Indian girls would come to me and ask about what they could do after they finished high school: what they could do on the reservation, what jobs they could get off the reservation. I hoped they would discuss their problems with me, what their goals should be. I'd be more than happy to talk with them. But I can't go to them and tell them what to do. Just because I've worked outside for three years doesn't give me the right to plan for other people. But I thought I had something to offer the girls here, if only they would come for advice.

I would like to see the financial records at the store so well kept that an accountant could come in at any time and check the books, and they would be in perfect order. It is difficult because only Louise and I can run the store, and if either of us gets sick, the other one has to be at the store from 7 AM to 9 PM, or else close the store. At first I had to be very patient with Louise and explain everything to her. She had no training at all. Sometimes I started to get mad when I explained and explained, but then I'd remember that she can't help it. People do not know some of the things I know, and I must not get irritated. But if things go wrong, I am responsible, and it is a big responsibility. The younger people are not exactly lazy; they just don't know how to work. I want them to work and be on time. If they need time off, they should tell me, not just go away or not appear on some days.

So some of them start calling me bossy. But that is my responsibility. I tried to talk to them and tell them why I wanted them to come to work on time, but still they didn't. I want them to realize that they have to work to earn their money. It is not a gift. They were supposed to do something in return for their wages. They are interested in boys at their age, and that's why they aren't good workers. But still, the National Youth Corps, operating in Big Cypress, gives kids some idea of how it is to work, to have a job. If I don't make them do the job, they're really not earning their money. That is one thing I had to face. I know that they are going to say I'm mean and bossy. I expect that. But if I'm in charge, they're going to do what they're supposed to do. That's the way I look at it. Everybody talks here. I know that, but I've been away, and I can take it.

I think people my own age are jealous. It is not shyness. Before I left, they were all friendly to me. I came back, and they all look at me, but when I go to talk to them, they just turn around, and it is so hard for me. They answer me, but they don't answer like they used to, and talk to me. That has been my main problem. It is hard for someone to come back, but if he is strong enough, you know, he can go ahead and take that. Maybe some day people will understand. There is no reason to come back if you really think you are better than the people. They are wrong if that is what they believe about me. There is not enough money here, and if I didn't really care about the people, then I would have no reason to return.

I am worried about my mother, and I want to stay where I can help her (my parents are now divorced). It is best to come back and act like the other people, dress like they dress, try to be a part of them again. So even if a person didn't have kinfolk here, if he wanted to help, he could. But he must not show off or try to appear better.

If I didn't have a family here, it would be almost like going to live with strangers. I have to work now. It has become a part of my life. People here just don't understand that. I can't just sit around or visit and do nothing.

If there were no work here, I could not live here. It would be so hard for me to live the way the women here do, sewing all the time or working in the fields, but if I had to take care of my family and there was nothing else to do, I guess I would stay here for that. My aunt has taught me to do the traditional sewing, and how to make the dolls, so I could earn money doing that; but I wouldn't do it unless I had to stay here to take care of my family.

I think the reason almost all the educated Indians are girls is because a woman's life here on the reservation is harder than the man's. The women have to take all the responsibility for everything. To go to school and get a job is really easier for a woman than staying on the reservation. The men on the reservation can just lay around all day and go hunting. They can work for a little while on the plantations if they need a little money. But the women have to worry about the children. If the women go away and get jobs, then the men have to take responsibility.

A woman and a man should have about the same amount of education when they marry. That means there is no one at Big Cypress I can marry. The boys my age here do not have anything in common with me. If a girl marries an outsider, she has to move away, because the Tribal Council has voted that no white man can live on the reservation. A woman probably would miss the closeness of her family on the reservation. I would want to come back and visit, but I think I could marry out and make it successful. I would expect to meet and know his family. I would like to live near our families, if possible. I will always feel close to my family.

Sometimes I think about the city and all the things to do there. Then I remember my mother and how she is weak and needs someone who will watch over her and help her.

You know my mother drinks a lot. She is sick, and the doctors want her to stop; but she herself cannot control her drinking. Well, I guess us kids have shut our eyes, hoping things will get better by themselves. I know you have not heard this before, and I wish I was not the one to tell you this sad story, but my move back to the reservation was partly brought on because of this. She has been to a sanitarium where they help people like her. It has helped her already to know that I want to see her get help and be a better person. I am having a chickee built for her, and I must stay here until she is well enough to manage alone.

Economic opportunity has been severely limited on the reservation until recently. Employment for field hands or driving farm machinery has been available on ranches in the area, but the income is seasonal. Both men and women work at crafts. The products are sold either privately or through the Arts and Crafts Store at the tribal agency on the coast but the income is inadequate by itself. Some of the men and one or two Indian women own cattle, but none of these sources of income would appeal to a person with higher education. Until the opening of the grocery store, there was no job on the reservation which really required literacy, let alone a diploma.

Examining these possibilities and the words of Nellie Greene, what would entice an educated Indian to come back to work and live on the reservation? A good paying job; a high status as an educated or skilled person; to be back in a familiar, friendly community; a desire to be with his family and to help them. Perhaps for the rare individual, an earnest wish to try to help his own people. But income from a job on the reservation must allow a standard of living not too much lower than that previously enjoyed as a member of outer society. Nellie never gave any consideration to returning to the reservation until there was the possibility of a job that challenged her skills and promised a comparable income. The salary she receives from managing the store is close to what she had made at the bank in Miami. In Miami, however, she worked 40 hours a week, while on the reservation she works nearly 60 hours a week for approximately the same pay, because there are no trained personnel to share the responsibility. Given the isolation of Big Cypress, there is not enough time, after she has put in her hours at the store, to go anywhere off the reservation. It is not merely a question of total pay; it is a problem of access to a way of life unattainable on the reservation. Economic opportunity alone is not sufficient.

It is quite apparent from Nellie's interviews and from observation of the interaction between Nellie and other Indians, both in the store and elsewhere on the reservation, that her status is very low. Her position appears to vary: from some slight recognition that her training places her in a category by herself, to distinct jealousy, to apparent puzzlement on the part of some of the old folks as to just what her place in the society is. Through the whole gamut of reaction to Nellie, only her proud family considers her status a high one.

The primary reason Nellie gave for returning to the reservation was to help her people, but the reservation inhabitants did not indicate that they viewed her activities or presence as beneficial to them. Older Indians, both male and female, stated that it was "right" that she returned because Indians should stay together, not because she might help her people or set an example to inspire young

Indians who might otherwise be tempted to drop out of school. Younger people regard her as bossy and trying to act "white." She does not even have the status of a marriageable female. There is no Indian man on the reservation with the sort of background that would make him a desirable marriage partner, from her standpoint; in their traditional view of an ideal wife, she does not display the qualities preferred by the men. At the same time, there is a council ordinance which prohibits white men from living on the reservation, and therefore marriage to a white man would mean that she would have to leave the reservation to live. There is no recognized status of "career woman," educated Indian, or marriageable girl, or any traditional status for her.

Obviously, with an inferior status, it is unlikely that a person would perceive the community as a friendly, familiar environment. From the point of view of the reservation people, who have had contacts with her, she is no longer truly "Indian," but rather someone who has taken over so much of the Anglo-American ways as to have lost her identity as an Indian woman. Nearly all of Nellie's close acquaintances are living off the reservation. The only two girls she considers friends on the reservation are, like herself, young women with more than average contact with outside society, although with less formal education.

Nellie may have rationalized her decision to return by stressing her determination to help the people, but her personal concern for her mother probably influenced her decision to return more than she herself realized. Nellie was the only person in the family who had the ability, knowledge and willingness to see that her mother received the proper supervision and help.

The Bureau of Indian Affairs is attempting to increase the economic opportunities on the reservations, but I believe their efforts at holding back the "brain drain" of educated Indians will not be effective. Retraining the reservation people who do not have an education is certainly desirable. But, as the story of Nellie Greene points out, it takes more than good pay and rewarding work to keep the educated Indians down on the reservations. If the educated Indian expects to find status wtih his people, he is going to be disappointed. White people outside are apt to pay more attention to an educated Seminole than his own Indian society will. If the Indian returns from college and expects to find warm personal relationships with persons of his own or opposite sex, he is going to find little empathy, some distrust and jealousy because of his training and experiences outside the reservation. For Nellie Greene there was a personal goal, helping her sick mother. She was lucky to find a job that required her skills as an educated person, and which paid her as well as the bank at Miami. Her other goal, to help her own people, was thwarted rather than helped by her college education.

February 1970

Mexican Americans: The Road to Huelga

JOHN R. HOWARD

The basic demographic facts on Mexican Americans are as follows: In 1960 there were about three and a half million persons with Spanish surnames living in the southwest.

• Occupationally, they clustered toward the lower end of the scale, less than 5 percent of the males having professional or technical jobs. Better than 40 percent were laborers.

• Their median annual income was about two-thirds that of whites. In 1960, 31 percent of Mexican-American families earned less than $3,000 a year.

• The average Mexican American male had completed 8.1 years of schooling. Among urban males 14 years of age and over, 16 percent had less than five years of schooling.

• About 80 percent are found in urban areas. Indices of residential segregation in southwestern and western cities reveal Mexican Americans to be less segregated than blacks but to cluster nevertheless in distinct communities.

Some Mexican Americans in the Southwest are descendants of people who lived in the area before it was acquired by the United States; the bulk, however, are descendants of Mexicans who migrated to this country in the twentieth century.

Mexican Americans are what has been termed in the Introduction "a partial minority group." They have high visibility and a distinct social status only in parts of the country. Over much of the country their ethnic identity has low salience. In the Southwest where they concentrate in large numbers they have long had the status of a minority group. Historically, they have been subjected to racial discrimination and economic exploitation. Gamio caught some of the ambiguity of their status in the 1920s.

"The darkest skinned Mexican experiences almost the same restriction as the Negro, while a person of medium dark skin can enter a second-class restaurant. A Mexican of light brown skin as a rule will not be admitted to a high-class hotel, while a white, cultured Mexican will be freely admitted to the same hotel, especially if he speaks English fluently."

Paul Taylor, of the University of California, referring to the same period, quoted a waitress who articulated even finer distinctions. "We serve Mexicans at the fountain but not at the tables. We have got to make some distinction between them and the white people. The Negroes we serve only cones."

Segregation of Mexican Americans in the public school system was practiced until the end of World War II. School codes in California permitted the segregation of "Indian children or children of Chinese, Japanese, or Mongolian descent." Nothing was said about Mexican-American children, but they were segregated anyway. Ironically, a case involving Mexican-American children foreshadowed the *Brown* vs *Board of Education* Supreme Court ruling against segregation of black children. In a decision handed down on March 21, 1945, Judge Paul J. McCormick ruled that segregation of Mexican-American children found no sanction under California law and that it violated the "equal protection" clause of the Fourteenth Amendment.

Discrimination extended to employment. Carey McWilliams in *North From Mexico* contended in 1949 that "The biggest factor retarding the assimilation of the Mexican immigrant . . . has been the pattern of his employment . . . it is not the individual who has been employed but the group. . . . The jobs for which Mexicans were employed en masse had certain basic characteristics; they were undesirable by location (such as section-hand jobs on the desert sections of the rail lines, or unskilled labor in desert mines and cement plants); they were often dead-end types of employment, and the employment was often seasonal or casual."

Hostility toward Mexican Americans has persisted. Many Anglos express support for egalitarianism in the abstract, but when asked about specifics their responses indicate prejudice. Data gathered by Pinkney in Bakersfield, California early in the 1960s indicated only 6 percent of Anglo respondents expressing dislike of Mexicans. They displayed considerable hostility however when asked about specifics such as integrated housing, joint membership in clubs, and equal employment opportunities. They were least opposed to nondiscriminatory employment and most opposed to mixed housing, only 38 percent agreeing that Mexicans "should have the right to live with other Americans."

Discrimination is often subtle. Theodore Parsons in a 1966 Stanford University doctoral thesis cited examples drawn from 40 days of observing classes in a San Joaquin Valley elementary school with 58 percent Mexican-American enrollment. One teacher explained why he asked an Anglo boy to lead five Mexican Americans in orderly file out of the room by saying, "His father owns one of the big farms in the area and one day he will have to know how to handle Mexicans." Another teacher explained the practice of calling on Anglo pupils to help Mexicans recite by stating that, "It draws them (the Anglos) out and gives them a feeling of importance."

At least three factors account for the persistence of the Mexican American's status problems. Below these are enlarged upon.

The Conquered Provinces

McWilliams observed about Mexican Americans that " . . . they are more like the typical minority in Europe than like the typical European minority in the United States. Mexicans were annexed by conquest along with the territory they occupied. . . . About the closest parallel that can be found in this hemisphere for the Mexican-minority is that of the French-Canadians in Quebec. . . . Like the Mexicans, the French-Canadians were 'here first.' . . . The parallel would be closer, of course, if the Province of Quebec were part of the United States. Then New Mexico could be regarded as the Quebec of the Mexicano."

Over a period of a dozen years Mexico lost an enormous amount of territory to the United States as a consequence of military defeat. The treaty of Guadalupe-Hidalgo ceded to the United States all Mexican territory north of the Rio Grande. Ironically, the gold that Spanish adventurers from Cortes to Coronado to Onate had sought was discovered in California nine days before the treaty was signed, unbeknownst to its signers. The Gadsden purchase added additional Mexican Territory. Most of the Mexicans living in the ceded territories chose to remain and accept American citizenship.

While guaranteed rights of citizenship by the treaty, Mexicans quickly became the victims of Anglo animosity. They were, of course, not simply a conquered people, but a conquered people who differed in culture, religion, and ethnicity from their conquerers. The early 1840s had seen the rise of the anti-Catholic Native American Party in the United States. Some of this anti-Popery found expression in the war against Catholic Mexico.

The Mexicans living in the ceded territories were, if not non-white, at least less white than their conquerers. Many were of mixed Indian ancestry.

Mexicans, in short, were different in a sufficient number of ways as to make easy the formulation of rationalizations for the deprivations visited upon them. Once established, systems of oppression have a tendency to become self-perpetrating as one group always benefits psychologically or materially from the depressed status and restricted opportunities of another group.

Mexicans fell victim early and inevitably to Anglo lust for their land. Under the treaty, Mexicans who remained in the ceded territory were guaranteed "free enjoyment of their liberty and property." In California, however, Mexican landowners were systematically expropriated through a combination of force and chicanery. Typically, there were large ranches on the sites of what are now some of the major cities in the state: Oakland, San Diego, Los Angeles. With greater or lesser degrees of rapidity, Anglo squatters appropriated the land owned by the Peraltas, the Berreyesas, and other prominent Mexican families. Some families fought back with arms, most became entangled in legal battles that dragged on for years, ending with the original owners landless and destitute.

The subordinate status of the Hispanos and of later Mexican immigrants found expression in the vitality of certain stereotypes. Race prejudice was circulated as scientific dogma in the early decades of the century; R.L. Adams of the University of California, in his text *Farm Management*, stated that Mexicans were "childish, lazy and unambitious." He argued that as farm laborers they should be segregated from the Japanese who were "tricky," and both should be kept separate from Negroes given that they were "notorious Prevaricators . . . constantly annexing to themselves such minor things as chickens, lines from harnesses, axes and shovels."

Simmons, writing in 1961, indicated that the south Texas stereotype of Mexicans pictured them as improvident, undependable, childlike, and indolent. They were also believed to be dirty, drunken, and criminally-inclined.

Mexican-Americans, like blacks, have been a visible minority. They have had their opportunities curtailed and their civil liberties circumscribed. Most have accommodated themselves to subordinate status; however, there has been a persistent strain of protest. Let us discuss this protest in terms of the historical context out of which *La Causa* has grown.

From Banditry to La Causa

The initial overt reaction of the Hispanos to Anglo incursions was banditry. Leanard Pitt in *The Decline of the Californios* indicates that "For many Spanish American youths California represented a place that had robbed them of their birthright, but had meanwhile provided innumerable opportunities to steal back part of it. . . . Their forte was highway robbery, stage holdups, and rustling, activities in which they surpassed all other nationalities even after the gold rush. As late as 1875 the most notorious characters in the state wore sombreros."

Banditry is an individual response to social dislocation and may enrich the individual, but inevitably, has little consequence in changing a group's status. Organized Mexican-American protest has been centered largely, though not entirely, among arrgricultural workers. The roots of the Chicano movement lie in the fields.

Immigration of Mexicans in substantial numbers began in the first decade of this century and many of them were farm laborers; Mexican labor had been used before World War I, but during the war the big influx began. Mexicans in groups of 1,500 to 2,500 were brought into the Imperial Valley by truck from San Felipe and Guaymas. During the 1920s Mexicans were the largest single population group among the 200,000 agricultural workers in California. *The Pacific Rural Express* indicated that between 1924 and 1930 an average of 58,000 Mexicans a year were brought into the state to work in the fields.

As early as 1903 Mexican and Japanese sugar-beet workers went on strike in Ventura, California. In 1922 Mexican-American field hands sought to establish a union of grape-pickers at Fresno. In November 1927, a Confederation of Mexican Labor Unions was organized in Los Angeles and in April of 1928 efforts were made to organize cantaloupe pickers in the Imperial Valley. The growers reacted quickly. Mass arrests were made, deportations took place, and scabs were brought in from Texas and Oklahoma. The strikes were broken.

Two years later 5,000 Mexican-American agricultural workers struck. After a temporary settlement, growers again counterattacked successfully with mass arrests.

In June of 1933, 7,000 Mexican workers struck in Los Angeles County, walking out of berry, onion, and celery fields in the longest strike the state had seen until then. In the Fall of 1933 the militant Cannery and Agricultural Workers Union called a series of strikes attempting to organize the largely Mexican-American field hands in the southern San Joaquin Valley.

Not all protest occurred in California. Mexican-American farm laborers struck in Arizona, Idaho, Washington, and Colorado. A fifty-car caravan of workers toured the lower Rio Grande Valley in 1933 in protests against anti-union activity. In 1934, 6,000 pecan shellers struck in San Antonio against piece rates of two and three cents a pound.

Mexican-American protest, then, is not new, but *La Causa* is. In the fall of 1965 a bitter strike broke out in the grape vineyards surrounding the little central California town of Delano. The strike was led by former agricultural worker and community organizer Cesar Chavez and his National Farm Workers' Association. The strikers focused on bread-and-butter issues, the ·average annual income of Mexican-American farm laborers being $1,378. Unlike previous protest efforts however the strike seemed to infuse the population with a spirit of militancy. Eventually *Huelga,* the strike, became *La Causa,* a crusade to assert the dignity of the Mexican-American population.

Earlier efforts to organize had met with limited success. The AFL-CIO set up the Agricultural Workers Organizing Committee in the 1950s. Due, in part, to the fact that its leadership was Anglo and had little grasp of Mexican culture, AWOC never solidly established itself with Mexican workers. Additionally, there were certain standard problems in organizing farm workers. Galarza listed these: "Farm wages are so low that the monthly union dues seem a heavy tax on the workers. There are long periods of unemployment when union obligations can be met only at considerable sacrifice. A trade union of farm workers must face and meet assaults on its security ranging from local irritation, through state legislative attacks, and up to international maneuvers to swamp local living and working standards."

The Community Service Organization made the most important attempt to organize the urban Mexican community. CSO was the inspiration of Saul Alinsky, a professional in the business of organizing the powerless. Alinsky set forth his philosophy in *Reveille for Radicals,* arguing that "people's organization" had to be established to ensure that the interests of non-elites are represented in the councils of power. CSO undertook voter registration campaigns among Mexicans. "Through the CSO, the Mexican-Americans began to take action, first on such bread and butter items as better sewage disposal and new sidewalks, and then through the ballot box. . . ." Early in the 1960s Cesar Chavez, who had become General Director of CSO, put forth a proposal to organize farm laborers. The urban oriented CSO found this too parochial, and voted it down at its 1962 convention. Whereupon Chavez quit the organization, moved to Delano, California, and set about organizing.

At least three factors account for the unprecedented impact of the Chavez movement. First, as regards the farm labor situation itself, the termination of the *bracero* program stabilized the labor force in the fields and denied growers a prime source of scab labor. In 1942 the Mexican and American governments had entered into an agreement allowing the recruitment of *braceros* or Mexican nationals as farm workers, their tenure in the United States being for the duration of their employment. Galarza commented that "these agreements were originally signed as a wartime measure, but they were continued under the insistent pressure of the agricultural employers' association who were looking for a counterpoise to the wage demands of Mexican workers long resident in this country." The end of the bracero program in 1964 removed from the hands of growers an important instrument for breaking strikes.

Second, the black protest movement had both generated consciousness of the possibility of reform and created a corps of young activists who supplied important knowhow and manpower for poor people attemping to organize on a mass basis. Available in 1965 were thousands of young whites, veterans of Mississippi and the civil rights movement. This corp of veterans proved invaluable in the early days of the strike.

Third, leadership of La Huelga was Mexican-American. Earlier organizations such as Citizens for Farm Labor were made up almost entirely of Anglos, and although they had spoken on behalf of the Mexican-American population they had no roots in that community.

A combination of circumstances, then, created the conditions under which an effective protest movement could come into existence.

La Huelga

The strike began largely by accident. In the spring of 1965, Filipino and Mexican-American workers in the Coachello Valley south of Delano had gone out on strike for higher pay. After ten days they went back to work for $1.40 an hour, a raise of 20 to 30 cents over their previous wage. Drifting north to Delano with the crops, they were reluctant to take lower wages than they had received in Coachello. On September 8, the Filipinos struck. Chavez later commented, "That morning of September 8, a strike was the furthest thing from my mind. . . . The first I heard of it was when people came to me and said the Filipinos had gone out. They were mad that the Filipinos weren't working and the Mexicans were. All I could think of was 'Oh God, we're not ready for a strike.' "

AWOC was supporting the strike of the Filipinos and sought the aid of the NFWA with whom it had never been on good terms. Feeling that the credibility of his organization would be severely impaired if he did not support the strike Chavez decided to go along. On Monday, September 20, with less than $100 in its strike treasury, the NFWA joined AWOC on the picket lines. As a majority of the strikers were now Mexican, leadership passed into Chavez' hands.

Chavez moved immediately to enlist the support of civil rights people and the liberal clergy. This served both to make the struggle more than a localized affair known only to people living in the area and to open up access to the desperately needed resources to keep a strike going. The trade union movement contributed a certain amount of money but it was not nearly enough. By the summer of 1966 the telephone bill of the NFWA was running $1,600 a month and gasoline was costing $4,000. The organization absorbed all of the expenses including rent, food, and car payments of the families on permanent picket duty. There was need of enough food to sustain strikers and their families, the weekly amounts running to 200 pounds of tortilla flour, 100 pounds of dry red beans, 100 pounds of pinto beans, 200 pounds of sugar, 200 pounds of potatoes, 50 pounds of coffee, two cases of canned fruits and vegetables, and enough powdered and canned milk for 450 children.

The young people who went to Delano proved invaluable

in organizing the support of the liberal and radical communities in California and eventually across the nation. Predictably the local community was hostile to the strike and the strikers. There were reflex comments about "communists" and "outside agitators." Nevertheless, an impressive support structure from outside the community sustained the strike.

The situation was rather complicated. There were more than 30 growers in the area, some independent operators, others connected with national enterprises such as Schenley and DiGiorgio, the latter turning out S&W and Tree Sweet canned food and fruit products.

Ultimately, any strike is a test of strength. Ironically, the weak, struggling NFWA, making its way with donated biscuits and amateur organizers, found the largest and most powerful of its opponents to be the most vulnerable. As national enterprises, Schenley and DiGiorgio were susceptible to a national protest movement. Additionally, having dealings with a number of unions, they were probably less prone than more parochial growers to see unions as evil incarnate. It is impossible to judge whether they were better able to settle financially, given that claims and counterclaims about the economic effects of agricultural worker unionization have never been satisfactorily evaluated.

The boycott was launched with an élan born of having little else to throw into the fray. Chavez indicated his reason for singling out Schenley. "It was simple decision. In the first place, booze is easier to boycott. And then it is usually the man who goes to the liquor store and he's more sympathetic to labor as a rule than his wife."

John Gregory Dunne recounted the launching of the crusade. "From an atlas, Chavez picked thirteen major cities across the United States as boycott centers, and then raised a boycott staff, all under twenty-five, from workers and volunteers who had impressed him on the picket line. They left Delano penniless and hitchhiked or rode the rails to the various cities where they were to set up shop. Chavez gave the boycott staff no money, both out of necessity and to prove a theory. He reasoned that if a person could not put his hands on enough money to maintain himself on a subsistence level, then he would be of little use raising money for the boycott and setting up an organization."

The boycott staff contacted liberal clergy, radicals, union leaders and others in each city likely to listen and lend help. In New York the Transport Workers Union assisted in printing and distributing leaflets to subway riders. A Boston Grape Party was staged in Boston, marchers winding through the city with crates of Delano grapes, which were then dumped in the harbor.

Schenley settled on April 6, 1966, seven months after the strike had begun. The circumstances attending the decision are still not clear. Some claim fear of an effective boycott, others suggest an unfounded fear of a bartenders' boycott of Schenley products.

The struggle against DiGiorgio proved more complicated. Unlike Schenley the DiGiorgio firm had been in the agriculture business a long time and was as practiced at breaking strikes as it was at merchandising its food and fruit products. In 1939, 1947, and 1960 it had defeated attempts at organization on the part of its workers. The national attention given the grape strike and the wide base of support accorded the strikers this time, however, faced the corporate giant with a much more demanding situation.

The already muddy situation became muddier when the Teamsters' Union began to evince interest in organizing farm laborers. Teamster interest was partially a consequence of an internal struggle for power among possible successors to James Hoffa, who was attempting to stay out of jail. Di-Giorgio was interested in doing business with the Teamsters out of spite for the NFWA and possibly in the belief that a better deal could be made with them. A summer of bitter conflict culminated in an NFWA victory of 530 to 331 over the Teamsters in an election to determine which union would represent field workers. The Teamsters won the shed workers' vote 94 to 43.

Further negotiations finally brought a specific settlement The contract provided for a union shop, a minimum wage of \$1.65 an hour, a guarantee of four hours "reporting and standby" pay if no work was available, and a week's paid vacation for those employed more than 1,600 hours a year. The minimum wage was to be raised to \$1.70 an hour in 1968 with two weeks paid vacation for workers who had been with DiGiorgio for three years.

These victories in the first year of the struggle helped transform *La Huelga* into *La Causa*. A dispute over the wages of agricultural workers was generalized into a movement to redefine the status of an entire group.

The Brown Power Movement

The long-range impact of the farm workers' revolt will probably lie in the cities rather than in the fields. Mechanization on the farm has decreased the need for agricultural workers. The trend is widespread. Mechanization in Hawaii, for example, reduced the work force in island sugar from 35,000 in 1945 to 10,500 in 1966. The United Farm Workers Organizing Committee (the successor to the NFWA) claimed 17,000 members in California and the southwest in 1967. The bulk of the Mexican population, however, lies in the city. *La Huelga* served as a catalyst to change.

Today there are many faces to the Brown Power movement. The article in this volume deals with Tijerina and a kind of nationalist rennaissance among Mexicans in New Mexico. "Corky" Gonzalez in Denver has addressed a different set of problems. And in California Chavez continues the fight, many growers still resisting unionization. Mexicans have joined in demands on California campuses for "Third World" and ethnic studies programs.

The thrust and direction of the Brown Power movement are not yet clear, but, as with the Black Power movement it marks a significant change in the nature of contemporary majority-minority relations.

FURTHER READING

Reveille for Radicals by Saul D. Alinsky (Chicago; University of Chicago Press, 1946) is a handbook for community organizers of a radical pursuation, by an old-time radical and community organizer.

Delano: The Story of the California Grape Strike by John Gregory Dunne (New York; Farrar, Straus & Giroux, 1967) is a journalistic recounting of the events leading up to the strike and of the first year of the strike.

Mexican American Youth by Celia S. Heller (New York; Random House, 1966) is a good little book on a neglected portion of the nation's population of young people.

Factories in the Field by Carey McWilliams (Archon Books, 1969) is a classic on the problems and protests of agricultural workers.

North From Mexico by Carey McWilliams (Philadelphia and New York; J.P. Lippincott Company, 1949) is an excellent treatment of the history and status of Mexican Americans through World War II.

The Decline of the Californios by Leonard Pitt (Berkeley and Los Angeles; University of California Press, 1966) describes the decline and fall of Mexicans in California between 1840 and 1900.

La Raza: The Mexican Americans by Stan Steiner (New York: Harper and Row, 1969), a social history of the rise of the Brown Power movement.

Mexican Labor in the United States: Migration Statistics by Paul S. Taylor (Berkeley; University of California Press, 1933) contains data on the volume of Mexican farm labor migration to the country during the 1920s and the patterns of dispersal of such labor in the country.

"The Mexican American: A National Concern" by Ernesto Galarza in *Race Prejudice and Discrimination,* Arnold Rose, editor (New York: Alfred A. Knopf, 1951) presents "Mexican Problem" during the 1940s?

"Prejudice Toward Mexican and Negro Americans: A Comparison" by Alphonse Pinkney in *Phylon* (First Quarter, 1963).

La Raza:
Mexican Americans
in Rebellion

JOSEPH L. LOVE

In early June, 1967 a group of Spanish-speaking Americans who call themselves the *Alianza Federal de Mercedes* (Federal Alliance of Land Grants) and claim that they are the legal and rightful owners of millions of acres of land in Central and Northern New Mexico, revolted against the governments of the United States of America, the State of New Mexico, and Rio Arriba (Up River) County, formally proclaiming the Republic of Rio Chama in that area.

On June 5 an armed band of forty or more *Aliancistas* attacked the Tierra Amarilla courthouse, released 11 of their members being held prisoner, and wounded a deputy sheriff and the jailer. They held the sheriff down on the floor with a rifle butt on his neck, searched for the District Attorney (who wasn't there) and for an hour and a half controlled the village (population 500). They took several hostages (later released when the getaway car stuck in the mud).

Despite some of the melodramatic and occasionally

comic opera aspects of the affair, both the members of the *Alianza* and the local and state authorities take it very seriously. This is not the first time the Aliancistas have violated federal and state law, attempting to appropriate government property (in October, 1966, for instance, their militants tried to take over Kit Carson National Forest, and to expel the rangers found there as trespassers) ; nor is it the only time their activities have resulted in violence. In this case the state government reacted frantically, sending in armored tanks, 300 National Guardsmen and 200 state police. They rounded up dozens of Spanish-speaking persons, including many women and children, and held them in a detention camp, surrounded with guns and soldiers, for 48 hours. The raiders got away, but in several days all of them—including their fiery leader, former Pentecostal preacher Reies López Tijerina—were captured.

It has become common to associate these actions of the Alianza with other riots or revolts by poor, dark-skinned and disaffected Americans—with Watts, Newark and Detroit. Tijerina himself helps reinforce this impression by occasionally meeting with, and using the rhetoric of, some leaders of the black urban revolt. The fact is, however, that the Alianza movement is really a unique example in the United States of a "primitive revolt" as defined by Eric Hobsbawm, a kind almost always associated with developing nations, rather than advanced industrialized countries —and which includes such diverse phenomena as peasant anarchism, banditry, and millenarianism (the belief that divine justice and retribution is on the side of the rebels and that the millenium is at hand). The attack on the courthouse, in fact, had more in common with the millenarian Sioux Ghost Dance cult of 1889-91 than with Watts.

As the Aliancistas see it, they are not violating any legitimate law. The territory around Rio Arriba belongs to them. They demand the return of lands—primarily common lands —taken from *Hispano* communities, most of which were founded in the Spanish colonial era. Their authority is the famous *Recopilación de leyes de los Reinos de Indias* (*Compilation of Laws of the Kingdoms of the Indies,* generally shortened to *The Laws of the Indies*) by which the Crown of Castile governed its New World possessions. They claim that according to these laws common lands were inalienable—could not be taken away. Since most of such lands were in existence when the Treaty of Guadalupe Hidalgo was signed in 1848—and since in that treaty the United States government pledged itself to respect property rights established under Mexican rule—the Alianza insists that those land grants remain valid. The members speak primarily of common lands, rather than individual heirs, and define the towns in question as "closed corporations, with membership restricted to the descendants and heirs of the founding fathers and mothers"—that is, themselves.

The Alianza's interpretations of law and history are, of course, selective, and tend to ignore inconvenient facts and other interpretations. It claims that *The Laws of the Indies* were not abrogated when "Mexico invaded and occupied New Mexico," nor when the United States did the same in 1846. The Aliancistas are the early settlers, the legitimate heirs.

The Alianza and its actions cannot really be understood without knowledge of its background and its leader. First, the people from whom it draws its members and its strength—the Mexican-American minority in the US—and specifically New Mexico; second, the rapid economic changes throughout the area since World War II that have so greatly affected their lives; and last but surely not least the dynamism, determination and charisma of Reies Tijerina, without whom the movement would probably never have arisen.

In the 1960 census Mexican-Americans, though they made up only 2.3 percent of the population of the United States, constituted 12 percent of the population of Texas,

New Mexico, Arizona, Colorado and California—almost three and a half million persons.

Generally they are a submerged minority that have only lately begun to articulate their demands. They formed "Viva Kennedy" committees in 1960; since then three Mexican-American Congressmen have gone to the House, and New Mexico's Joseph Montoya sits in the Senate. The end of the *bracero* program in 1964 opened the way to a successful unionization drive among agricultural workers; and the celebrated "Huelga" strike in Delano, California in 1965 was a symptom of and stimulus to the new awakening. The federal and state poverty programs, and the example of the Negro revolt, have also undoubtedly had their effects.

New Mexico is a distinctive area of Latin culture. It was the last state in the Southwest to be overwhelmed by Anglo-American civilization, and is the only one with two official languages. The Mexican-American population has been traditionally located along the Rio Grande and its tributaries, and extends into southern Colorado.

Until recent years, the Mexican Americans of New Mexico have been isolated from other members of *la raza* (the Mexican-American "race"). Texas and California have more than 80 percent of the Mexican-American population of the Southwest, yet most of these crossed over from Mexico after 1900, or descended from persons who did. But, the New Mexican *Hispanos* (the local name) have resided there for many generations, and some strains go back to the seventeenth century (Santa Fe was founded in 1609). Moreover, large numbers of English-speaking Americans only began to compete seriously for rural property in the 1880's, and appropriation continued into the 1920's.

In the 1960 census New Mexico had a higher percentage of "native born of native parents" than any other Southwestern state (87.4 percent). The mobility of Hispano males between 1955 and 1960 (defined in terms of changing residence) was lower in New Mexico than elsewhere.

In 1960 New Mexico had the highest percentage of rural non-farm inhabitants with Spanish surnames. In absolute numbers New Mexico's Anglo population was for many years roughly in balance with the Hispano. It is now surging ahead as a result of the economic boom which began with the atomic testing program of World War II. In no other Southwestern state was the disparity between the growth of Anglo and Latin populations greater from 1950 to 1960 than in New Mexico, where the former increased by 59.1 percent and the latter by a mere 8.1 percent. Yet in spite of this, New Mexico in 1960 still had a greater proportion of Mexican-Americans than any other state: about two-sevenths of its inhabitants had Spanish surnames, compared to one-seventh of Texans, and one-eleventh of Californians.

The job situation for the Hispanos of New Mexico has also worsened more rapidly than in other states. In 1950 male Mexican-Americans had a greater percentage of jobless in California, Colorado, and Arizona than in New Mexico; but ten years later the Hispanos of New Mexico had the dubious distinction of leading the list.

As some observers have noted, in certain ways New Mexico resembles Quebec: Both are centers of Latin culture founded in the seventeenth century, and both are subject to an increasing degree of Anglo domination. And like the Quebeckers, the New Mexicans have their fringe-group separatists—the *Alianza Federal de Mercedes.*

The Alianza was born in 1963, partly to combat the alienation and isolation of the Hispanos, but specifically to reclaim lands taken from the Spanish-speaking population since 1848. In colonial New Mexico (1598-1821), Spanish officials made land grants of indeterminate size to both individuals and to communities as commons, and the latter were respected through the era of Mexican rule (1821-1848). When Anglo-Americans began to enter New Mexico in significant numbers in the 1880's, they found it possible to wrest lands from the native inhabitants through the legal and financial devices of land taxes, mortgages, and litigation over disputed titles. By 1930, through legal and extralegal means, the Anglos had taken over most of the farming and ranching land in the state, and the state and federal governments appropriated much of the common lands that had previously belonged to the incorporated towns and villages. The Spanish-speaking population ultimately lost 1.7 million acres of community lands and two million acres in private holdings. The Hispanos sporadically reacted to this process by forming secret societies and vigilante groups; but at most this constituted harassment rather than effective resistance.

The Alianza now demands the return of these lands.

Yet in all probability, the Alianza would not exist but for the efforts of a single man, a leader who devotes his life to his cause, and inspires his followers to do likewise. Reies López Tijerina is a man of rare charisma who is most in his element when haranguing a large crowd. Of average height, he seems to have great physical strength as he grasps a microphone with one sinewy arm and gesticulates artfully and furiously with the other. He sometimes shouts violently as he asks rhetorical questions of his audience in Spanish—the language he uses by preference—and gets "Sí!" and "No!" bellowed back in appropriate cadences. The author witnessed a Tijerina performance last fall on the steps of the state capitol in Austin, Texas, where the Alianza leader told a group of Mexican-American Labor Day marchers he supported their demand for a state minimum wage of $1.25 an hour, but did so "with shame." Why should Mexican-Americans in Texas ask so little of the Anglos, whose government had repeatedly broken the Treaty of Guadalupe Hidalgo?

Reies Tijerina uses a demagogic style before a crowd, but he holds the tenets of his faith with unshakeable conviction: "It's something in me that must come out," Tijerina proclaims. His followers regard him with awe. He is "Caudillo" (leader) of the Alianza, but disclaims any desire to be dictator. He points out that a Supreme Council has ultimate control—though he, clearly, makes the decisions. It seems obvious that no one could step into his shoes, nor has anyone been groomed to do so. In any event Tijerina has no doubt that his followers require strong and able leadership. He justifies this by arguing that the Hispanos are a "young" race. They were "born," he explains, by virtue of a royal decree in 1514 allowing Spaniards to marry Indians; the term "Hispano" or "Spanish American" therefore can generally be equated with "mestizo." This young race is still learning, painfully, how to defend itself and requires strong direction. It is not an ancient and clever people like the Jews, he says.

Recognizing the diverse historical experiences of Texas, New Mexico, and California, the Caudillo realizes that his constituency for the foreseeable future will be limited to New Mexico. He does believe, however, that the land grants to Mexican-Americans in California can still be identified and claimed like those of New Mexico.

It is no coincidence that Tijerina's style and language recall Pentecostal protestantism. He has been a minister in the Assembly of God, and was an itinerant revival preacher for many years to Mexican-Americans throughout the Southwest.

But, unlike the vast majority of his followers, he was not born in New Mexico but in Texas ("A prophet is not without honor save in his own country"). One of seven children of a migrant farm family, once so desperate that they were reduced to eating field rats, he picked crops and preached in Illinois and Michigan as well as in Texas and Arizona. He did not settle in New Mexico until 1960; and, with his five brothers, formed the Alianza three years later.

The quasi-religious fervor of Tijerina has strongly shaped the aspirations and style of the Alianza. However, there is greater emphasis on Old Testament justice than New Testament love. *Justicia* is a word frequently on the Caudillo's lips.

The Alianza now claims to have 30,000 dues-paying members paying at least $2.00 per month. A scholar guesses that 10,000 may be closer to the true figure. It seems clear that Tijerina's computation includes sympathizers or at least persons who have only occasionally contributed funds.

As with some sectors of the American Negro movement, the Alianza's programs began with an emphasis on litigation; and when that failed, frustration and a disposition toward violence emerged.

In April 1966 the "President and Founder" of the Alianza journeyed to Spain in order to gather materials on the registration of New Mexican land grants in the colonial era; from such documents he hoped to generate a strong legal case to present in federal courts.

In July Tijerina presented a petition to the Governor of New Mexico, Jack Campbell, and stated, "We do not demand anything. We just want a full investigation of the issue." Yet Governor Campbell would do little more than receive Tijerina and hear him out.

In January 1967, the Caudillo, one of his brothers, and a self-styled legal expert in the Alianza named Gerry Noll made a trip to Washington, D.C., where they "limited" their claims to 500,000 acres in the Kit Carson National Forest and to an area around the city of Albuquerque. He only obtained a brief hearing with a State Department attorney and a sympathetic interview with New Mexico's Senator Montoya.

In 1966 the Alianza had already begun to give up hope of legal redress. The Supreme Council of the Alianza "passed a resolution of non-confidence in the Courts of the State of New Mexico and of the United States of America" because of "corruption" and "low standards of knowledge of law."

On October 22, 1966 the Aliancistas proclaimed the existence of the Republic of San Joaquín del Río de Chama (in Rio Arriba County) with Tijerina as "city attorney" *(procurador)* of the community; they simultaneously attempted to take over Kit Carson Forest, which covers most of the county. They arrested U.S. Forest Rangers for trespassing, decided to print hunting and fishing licenses, and commandeered government vehicles. The rebels were quickly dispersed by local authorities, and Tijerina and four lieutenants were charged on counts of assault, converting government property to private use, and conspiracy.

Demonstrations and protest meetings continued. On January 15, 1967 the Alianza declared it would seek redress in the United Nations if the U.S. Congress failed to act. On April 17 several hundred Aliancistas paraded before the State House in Santa Fe, and Reies Tijerina, out on bond, delivered an ominous message: "We will . . . issue to the public and the federal government and the world the last human legal notice exposing the truth. . . . The government is being warned and advised if anybody is found trespassing on these land grants they will be arrested and punished. . . ."

At the beginning of June the District Attorney of Santa Fe, Alfonso Sánchez, expressed concern about the "communist philosophy" of the Alianza and alleged that Aliancistas were amassing "machine guns, M-1 rifles, and 15,000 rounds" of ammunition. Eleven members of the Alianza were promptly arrested and jailed in Tierra Amarilla, an Alianza stronghold and the seat of Rio Arriba County.

The reaction was swift and violent: On June 5, as noted, the Aliancistas launched their revolt and attacked the Tierra Amarilla courthouse. This time, when caught, the Caudillo and his principal aides were charged with kidnapping, three counts of conspiracy to commit murder, and bombing a public building (the courthouse). Despite the gravity of the charges, Tijerina and some of his men were released on bond after six weeks in prison. The failure of the attack by no means dampened the spirits of the Aliancistas.

In the months following, Tijerina traveled throughout the Southwest to gain backing. He found it, both in radical organizations of Mexican-Americans and Negroes, and in some Mexican-American associations with more traditional reformist leadership.

On October 15, Tijerina was in Los Angeles, linking his cause to the peace movement at an anti-war rally. Labeling the United States' involvement in Vietnam "the most criminal in the history of mankind," he contacted radical Negro and Mexican-American groups in the Los Angeles area. One week later, at a convention of the Alianza de Mercedes on October 21, Tijerina announced that a "Treaty of Peace, Harmony, and Mutual Assistance" had been contracted between his organization and SNCC, CORE, and the Black Panthers. The Caudillo also obtained statements of support from the Crusade for Justice, a Mexican-American organization of slumdwellers in Denver, and from MAPA, an important Mexican-American political action group in California.

While gathering support from non-Anglo groups outside New Mexico in the here and now, Tijerina and his deputies have not discouraged the movement's latent tendencies toward millenarianism and belief in special divine favor back home on the Upper Rio Grande. During the raid at Tierra Amarilla, several Aliancistas witnessed the appearance of a double rainbow, a sure sign of God's grace. According to others, the Caudillo is the prophet of Montezuma who will miraculously return in the imminent future to punish the Anglos for their appropriation of Hispano lands.

Another legend has it that a leader will come "from the east" and expel the foreigners who took the Mexican-Americans' lands. (Tijerina fits, since Texas is east of New Mexico.)

In the *"Corrido de Rio Arriba,"* which appeared shortly

after the June raid, the balladeer told his audience that when bullets started flying *"Las mujeres y los niños/iban corriendo y llorando,*

Y en este instante pensamos/Que el mundo se iba acabando."

("Women and children / Ran about in tears And at that moment we thought / The world was coming to an end.")

Although the "free city-states" which Tijerina hopes to erect are of this world, they clearly represent a sort of secular paradise, a recaptured golden age, somewhat along the lines prescribed in *The Laws of the Indies.* The inhabitants will be able to do any work they please, explains the Caudillo; but most will be herdsmen using the common lands *(ejidos)* of the pueblos. Tijerina himself will simply become City Attorney of the Republic of Chama.

If "la raza" is specially favored and will come into its millenium, why is it suffering so now? This is explained as the result of a "fall from grace" which occurred after the Anglo-American invasion of New Mexico in 1846 and the collusion of certain Hispanos with the alien conquerors. An allegorical mural at Alianza headquarters tells the story: A sacred temple in the center of the mural represents paradise entwined by a serpent, which also clutches three figures symbolizing the oppressed races—the Negro, the Indian, and the Hispano. The snake personifies the "Santa Fe Ring"—the Anglo and upper-class Hispano politicians who appropriated the poor Hispanos' lands in the 1880's and later. Figures on the right side, representing the People, begin to emerge from the Darkness and a reptile-devouring secretary bird, personifying Justice, arrives to attack the snake. At the top of the canvas is a rainbow (a symbol of God's blessing) and the phrase "Justicia." Just below this emblem is the City of Justice, which will once more be reconstituted on earth.

Yet there is a sinister element in the apocalypse which

must precede the millenium: Anglos must be driven out. And Hispanos will be judged by whether they aided, stood aside from, or hindered the cause. Those who hindered will be treated harshly.

Gerry Noll, the Caudillo's lieutenant, has proclaimed as part of the Alianza creed:

. . . KNOW YE that We have exclusive and supreme jurisdiction within [New Mexico] over all persons and property situated therein. . . ."

We cannot afford to permit the present status quo to be maintained without actually destroying Our independence and autonomy. Consequently, We must take measures calculated to curtail the activities of any aggressors with the utmost dispatch . . . We shall enter troops into these territories to restore Our authority . . . woe to him who obeys the orders of the aggressor, for he shall be punished without mercy. . . .

THEREFORE KNOW YE that We shall commence to liberate Our kingdoms, realms, and dominions . . . We shall not take any prisoners of war, but shall take only war criminals and traitors and try [them] by a military tribunal and execute them.

At Tijerina's direction, the October 1967 convention of the Alianza unanimously set forth a weird dynastic claim: Gerry Noll was henceforth transformed into "Don Barne Quinto Cesar, King-Emperor of the Indies," the legitimate descendant of Ferdinand VII of Spain.

In November Tijerina, "Don Barne," and several other Aliancistas stood trial for the charges stemming from the invasion of Kit Carson Forest in 1966. During the trial it was revealed that Noll's real name was Gerald Wayne Barnes, convicted of bank robbery in 1945, grand larceny in 1949, forgery in 1953, and third-degree assault in 1963. Found guilty, Noll and Tijerina were sentenced to three and two years respectively. At the trial Don Barne declared, "I am willing to die for my country and for my people.

This is part of my job as king and all in a day's work."
When sentenced in mid-December he retorted to the court,
"It is I who make the laws—not the United States of
America."

While waiting trial on the multiple charges of the June
'67 raid and appealing against the decision in the first case,
Tijerina and his co-defendants were once more released on
bond. On January 3, 1968, again in Tierra Amarilla, Deputy Sheriff Eulogio Salazar was kidnapped and beaten to
death. Governor David Cargo, Campbell's successor, immediately revoked the bonds. Protests rapidly poured into
the Governor's office from SNCC, MAPA, and other organizations, and a short time later Tijerina was out on bail
again.

Since that time legal problems have necessarily absorbed
most of Tijerina's energies, as he appealed the verdict of
the first trial and prepared for the more serious set of
charges (including kidnapping) stemming from the Tierra
Amarilla affair. But the Caudillo found time to break into
national headlines again in May and June when he led his
followers at the Poor People's March on Washington. Al-
leging that the Negro leaders of the march refused to grant
Mexican-Americans an adequate place in the sun, Tijerina
cancelled Alianza participation in Resurrection City. Instead, he made use of his appearance in Washington to lec-
ture State Department officials on the meaning of the
Guadalupe Hidalgo Treaty—namely, the legitimacy of the
Spanish land grants.

Tijerina had hoped to run for governor in the November
1968 elections, but the New Mexico Supreme Court dis-
allowed his candidacy in October because of his conviction
the previous year. Meanwhile the second (Tierra Amarilla)
trial took place, during which Tijerina dramatically dismissed his lawyers and conducted his own defense. In mid-
December his self-confidence was justified by his acquittal
of kidnapping and two lesser counts. Other charges against

him and nine other defendants had yet to come before the courts at the end of 1968.

But the real historical and sociological meaning of the Alianza cannot be solely understood in terms of its current embroilments or recent history in New Mexico. Most of the literature on the movement, so far, has dealt with the spectacular, bizarre, or violent elements involved; but the roots of primitive revolt go far back.

Since the enclosure movement began in Europe in the twelfth century, there have been scores of peasant revolts. Many sought the restoration of common lands taken by nobles and gentry.

In medieval Spain, many villages owned herds and land in common, and a number of these arrangements survived as late as the Spanish Civil War. These towns had once enjoyed special legal sanctions called *fueros,* by which they could themselves decide whether or not to enforce royal decrees and pay taxes.

One historian has written that "The village communities spontaneously developed an extensive system of municipal services, to the point of their sometimes reaching an advanced stage of communism." A scheme was proposed in 1631 to "nationalize all pasturage and establish each peasant with sufficient head of sheep and cattle to support him." In 1633 the Crown tried to implement this project by regulating tenancy and fixing rents in perpetuity, making leases irrevocable and hereditary, and setting up regulation commissions. Though the plan failed, the demands of shepherds for adequate grazing land were part of the Hispanic tradition to which Tijerina appeals and went to Spain to study.

One student of Mexican-American culture, anthropologist Narcie González, writes that ". . . even now [1967] sheepherding remains an ideal way of life for the Hispano. . . . Virtually all contemporary accounts by social scientists comment upon the people's stated preference for this occupation. . . ." This preference explains why in Tijerina's Utopia the common lands are so highly valued. The Chama region, where the Tierra Amarilla revolt broke out, was principally a sheep-grazing area until after the Second World War.

What has occurred in New Mexico has been a breakdown of the traditional society, the ripping of the fabric of Hispano culture. In 1950, 41 percent of the Spanish-surname population in the state lived in urban areas; but by 1960, 61 percent did. Many of those moving to the cities (especially to Albuquerque) were ill prepared for their new way of life. In 1956 one investigator found that 834 out of 981 women in Albuquerque who received Aid to Dependent Children had Spanish surnames.

While the number of Anglo-Americans rapidly increased in New Mexico after World War II, the Mexican-American population was almost static, the high birth rate being offset by emigration to California. Consequently by 1960 the Anglo population in the state constituted almost two-thirds of the whole.

The legal structures of a modern capitalist society had by the late 1930's wrecked the traditional land-tenure patterns of the Upper Rio Grande. In 1940 Dr. George Sanchez reported that in Taos County "65 percent of the private lands represent land grants which have been subdivided or otherwise lost to the communities and families to which they were originally assigned. Of the original nine *mercedes* in Taos County, four were community grants and five were lands granted to individuals. . . . This cornerstone of Taos' economy has been destroyed by taxation and by uncontrolled exploitation." Furthermore, "Commercial livestock operators have acquired [the Hispano's] land grants and compete with him for grazing leases and permits on public lands. Exorbitant fees, taxes, and forced sales have crowded him out of his former grazing domain."

For a time the full impact of these changes were softened

by the booming war and atomic energy economy in New Mexico, and by the fact that the National Forest Service seems to have acted as a surrogate patrón for the Hispano shepherd. Until drought in the 1960's forced a cutback, the Hispano could still obtain the use of federal lands for pasturing his livestock.

Rio Arriba County was one of the areas least affected by the state's economic growth. In 1960 it had the highest percentage of rural non-farm population of all New Mexico's counties (91.3 percent). It ranked high in native-born inhabitants, and low in the percentage of migrants. It had the third lowest median education and the fifth lowest median family income. In Rio Arriba and the other northern counties where the Spanish-speaking population predominates, the average per capita income in 1967 was less than $1,000, compared to the state average of $2,310 and the national average of $2,940. Furthermore, according to Governor Cargo, "11,000 of 23,000 residents of Rio Arriba County are on welfare rolls." The 1960 census showed that county with the state's highest rate of unemployment— 15.1 percent—almost three times the state average.

But it is not only unemployment that makes the residents of Rio Arriba dependent on federal and state largesse —72.1 percent of all land still available for grazing is owned by the US government in Kit Carson Forest. And what the government grants, it can, and sometimes does, also refuse.

The disintegration of the traditional Hispano community seems well underway, and Tijerina articulates widely-shared feelings that his people do not want to assimilate into Anglo culture. He also rejects relief as demoralizing to its recipients, stating again and again, "We will no longer take powdered milk in exchange for justice." Recent increases in welfare assistance may actually have aggravated the situation by raising the Hispanos' hopes for greater improvement.

Reaction to social disintegration can take many forms, and the Hispanic religious tradition—plus Tijerina's own background as a Pentecostal preacher—have helped channel it into millenarianism. In the 1930's a religious group called the Allelujahs, an Hispano version of the Holy Rollers, became popular, and before it faded out as many as half the people of some northern New Mexico communities had joined, taking part in religious services in which "Passages from the Revelation of St. John are favorite texts [according to a 1937 report], and lead to frenzies of religious ecstasy." The Allelujah experience has helped prepare the ground. So perhaps have the *Penitentes,* a lay brotherhood of Hispano mystics and self-flagellants that traces its origins back to the colonial era.

When the Alianza failed to obtain redress through the courts, the hope for and belief in extra-legal and supernatural means of relief—natural enough in the presence of the charismatic and fiery Tijerina—became exacerbated. When the National Forest Service recently cut back the use of grazing lands because of drought, the Hispanos were the hardest hit—and Tijerina was at hand to transform frustration into action. The frequency of millenarianism when belief in and identity with the dominant society are lost has been well documented in sociological literature. The Alianza constitutes an almost classic case.

Yet there is a "modern" dimension to the Alianza, and this is a direct outgrowth of its appearance in an industrial society with rapid transcontinental communications and ever-vigilant news media. The Alianza fits the requirements of a "primitive rebellion" or "revitalization movement," but its links with urban radical and reformist groups outside New Mexico show its potential for evolving into something more modern. Thus there are two distinct dimensions of the movement—the "primitive," rural, grassroots constituency on the tributaries of the upper Rio Grande; and the "modern," urban, nationally-connected leadership in Albuquerque. The "visible" media-oriented sector is modern, but the "invisible" millenarian sector is not.

Tijerina's primary concern is still regaining lost community lands, as his action at the Poor People's March showed. The hunger for community lands—the *ejidos*—remains the basis for the "real" movement, despite manifestos of solidarity with the Black Panthers and denunciations of the war in Vietnam.

The ignorance of government officials of the basic nature of the movement is almost monumental. They tend to explain the Alianza away by easy, modern clichés. Some find in the references to common lands the spore of modern communism.

At the November 1967 trial, the prosecuting attorney declared, "This is not a social problem we're trying. This is a criminal problem." Even some sympathetic observers have used singularly inappropriate terms. Tom Wicker of the *New York Times* and Congressman Joseph Resnick, chairman of the House Agriculture Subcommittee on Rural Development, have both referred to Rio Arriba County as a "rural Watts."

But Rio Arriba has little in common with Watts. The majority of Aliancistas, the rural grassroots, are not industrial proletarians but primitive rebels—peasants reacting and striking back in millenarian fashion against the modernization that is tearing their society apart.

February 1969

Puerto Ricans:
The Making of a Minority Group

JOHN R. HOWARD

The United States acquired Puerto Rico at the turn of the century as a by-product of the war with Spain. Cuba was the major preoccupation in the conflict, but with the bloodless seizure of Puerto Rico, the nation found itself in possession of a pleasant Caribbean Island about the size of Connecticut with a population of nearly one million. During World War I, citizenship was conferred on the island's people.

The effects of continental control on the islanders were varied. In the first three decades of this century the death rate was reduced by half, the birth rate rose, and the population doubled. On the other hand, the island was virtually turned into a sugar plantation. Within four decades the sugar industry accounted for 40 percent of employment and 60 percent of exports. Profits, however, accrued to 8,000 entrepreneurs and the island was known as "Uncle Sam's sweatshop." A host of statistics defined the deprivation of the population. By 1930 the infant mortality rate was twice the continental average. According to McWilliams "nearly 90 percent of the rural population and about 40 percent of the urban population were suffering from hookworm; diarrhea and enteritis were responsible for about 35 percent of all infant deaths."

Migration patterns have fluctuated with economic changes on the island and on the mainland. Sporadic but unsuccessful attempts were made very early to recruit Puerto Rican farm laborers. In 1900, 5,000 laborers were brought to Hawaii to work in the sugar cane fields and another 1,500 were recruited to Arizona in 1926 to work in the cotton fields. Whatever the reason, these attempts were not successful, and New York City became the center of Puerto Rican immigration. There had been a tiny Puerto Rican community in the city as early as 1838, a Spanish Benevolent Society having been formed for their compatriots who were in need. The city had "500 persons of Puerto Rican birth in 1910, 7,000 in 1920, 45,000 in 1930."

Two factors combined to promote immigration to New York City; first, the degree of "racial" discrimination encountered in the city was less than that experienced in other parts of the country, and, second, the 1924 Immigration Act shut off the influx of workers from Europe and created a demand for new sources of labor on the part of the needle trades. As early as 1919, 130 Puerto Ricans were sent to Brooklyn by the island Immigration Bureau to work in a cortage factory. Between 1921 and 1930 immigration from the island increased substantially. The migrants were mostly young, mostly urban, and relatively more skilled than nonmigrants. For the most part family groups came.

During the worst years of the depression more people returned to the island than came to the continent. Following World War II migration increased sharply, averaging 50,000 a year in the first decade after the war. According to Padilla, "Over a period of years statisticians observed a mathematical correlation of .82 between net migration from Puerto Rico and national income in the United States. This high correlation has linked Puerto Rican migration out of the island with favorable business and employment conditions in the United States. In turn, throughout periods of economic recession in the United States, many Puerto Ricans have returned to the island."

By 1960 there were 613,000 first- and second-generation Puerto Ricans in the city and by 1970 the number was probably close to one million.

West Side Story

In the late 1950s a musical called *West Side Story* opened on Broadway. It was an updated version of Romeo and Juliet and dealt with a romance between an Anglo boy and a Puerto Rican girl played against the background of conflict between Puerto Rican and Anglo delinquent gangs. In a sense, *West Side Story* marked the coming of age of Puerto Ricans as a minority group. Their status was sufficiently "real" to be the key plot element in popular entertainment.

The West Side of *West Side Story* referred to the area of Manhattan bounded North and South by 130th Street and 96th Street and East and West by the East River and Central Park, "Spanish Harlem," "El Barrio," "Island in the City." Actually the musical should have been called East Side Story. The area was dominated by Italians through the end of World War II. By 1950, 30 percent of its population was Puerto Rican and by 1960 over 40 percent. From Spanish Harlem, Puerto Ricans have spread out to the other boroughs with the concentration in the Bronx being sufficiently

large as to be instrumental in the election of a Puerto
Rican borough president, Herman Badillo.

El Barrio is a classic American slum. The statistics define
only part of the reality, however; patterns of social organization and a certain cultural perspective define the other. Below each of these is discussed.

Puerto Ricans are at the bottom of the economic ladder
among the city's ethnic groups. In the late 1960s whites
earned close to $8,000 a year, nonwhite families (princi-
pally black) earned close to $5,000, while Puerto Rican
families made just under $4,000.

In other respects Puerto Ricans were in more straight-
ened circumstances than blacks. Herbert Bienstock, regional
director of the Bureau of Labor Statistics, indicated that 36.9
percent of Puerto Rican workers in East Harlem in 1968
were unemployed or underemployed. The rate for blacks
was lower. In Brooklyn's Bedford-Stuyvesant section the
unemployment rate among Puerto Ricans was 29.7 and 27.6
among blacks. The Puerto Rican unemployment rate was
12 percent in Harlem while 8 percent of blacks were unemployed.

"About half of all private dwellings in East Harlem are
delapidated. Almost one in three is overcrowded." Tuberculosis rates and venereal disease rates are high. One pregnant woman in three gets no prenatal care and the infant
mortality rate is 37 per 1,000 live births as compared to a
city average of 26 per 1,000 live births. While 38 percent
of blacks and 64 percent of the whites in East Harlem
owned their own homes in 1960, few Puerto Ricans did.
One in three of East Harlem's Puerto Ricans lives in a
"project." Projects are high-rise public housing developments. There are nine in East Harlem.

East Harlem's schools are slum schools. Patricia Sexton,

who did a pioneering study of social class and education in Detroit, commented on them in 1965: "In recent years 57 percent of East Harlem's school teachers had permanent licenses, 25 percent were substitutes, 18 percent had probationary licenses. In junior high 44 percent had permanent licenses and 43 percent were substitutes. Many licensed teachers in junior high taught subjects they were not licensed to teach. Many with only elementary licenses were teaching in junior highs."

Reading and IQ scores decline for East Harlem children the longer they stay in school. Sexton indicated that, "In the third grade, students in one district scored 2.8 on a reading test compared with the city average of 3.5. By the eighth grade, the East Harlem students were two full years below grade level . . . . By the eighth grade their IQ score was 83.2, compared with 103.4 for the city. In the third grade it had been 91.2, compared with 98.8 for the city . . . . In the junior high schools, 12 percent of students were reading above grade level, 8 percent on grade level, 10 percent one year below grade level, and 70 percent more than one year below grade level."

Most of the Puerto Ricans who do graduate from high school receive a general diploma, 8 percent a vocational degree, and 1.2 percent an academic diploma facilitating entrance to college.

Statistically, the problems of Spanish Harlem and Black Harlem are very similar. There are differences, however, with regard to style of life and cultural outlook. Puerto Ricans brought with them to the mainland a nominal Catholicism, a strong belief in a double standard of behavior for the sexes, and certain patterns of extended family organization.

The journalist Peter Hamill has commented on religion,

indicating that "it doesn't seem very strong anymore . . . .
Some 85 percent of the Puerto Ricans in Puerto Rico are
Catholics, but until very recently the church there was run
by outsiders, by Irish bishops or Spanish bishops, by anyone but Puerto Rican bishops. In New York this meant
that not many Puerto Ricans ever went to church, and those
that 'got religion' generally ended up in a more lively, less
authoritarian, but somewhat more puritanical form of
Christianity like the Pentecostal."

It is difficult to say to what extent Puerto Ricans remained oriented to the island. There was a good deal of
travel back and forth, which partially accounted for the low
degree of involvement in mainland politics. For whatever
reasons, the end of the 1960s saw a rise in political consciousness among Puerto Ricans. The Puerto Rican Bronx
borough president ran a strong third in the democratic
mayoralty primary of 1969. Redistricting promises a Puerto
Rican congressman in 1970 or 1972.

The Puerto Ricans came seeking a better life. For many
the reality is El Barrio. Puerto Rican experiences have been
similar in certain respects to those of other immigrant
groups, but the factors which denied them the stereotypic
assimilation process have yielded them their status as a
minority group.

Below, these factors are discussed.

The Making of a Minority Group

In some ways the history of Puerto Rican immigrants
parallels that of other groups. The West European Jew who
settled in the United States prior to the great wave of immigration of East European Jews tended to look with dis-
favor on the newcomers, feeling that their behavior and appearance lent credibility to the antisemitic stereotype.
Similarly, the small number of Puerto Ricans resident in

New York prior to mass immigration to the mainland felt themselves not to be victimized by prejudice and were critical of the migrants. Brown commented on this, "Since the immigration of Puerto Ricans became a reality in 1928, conditions have changed in New York. Those who came here twenty years ago have seen a marked change in the attitude of the continental. An old resident of a Puerto Rican barrio, among those expressing this view, said that twenty years ago, one could say with pride: 'I am a Spaniard or Puerto Rican and the people would be courteous to you. It is a very different situation now.'"

Hamill has also noted this. "A Puerto Rican was something strange and exotic in those days. There weren't enough of them to be a threat to anybody, not enough of them to be identified as a group. The word 'spic' came later (most common theory; from the phrase 'No spik Inglis'). It came with the wave after the war. It came with the airplane."

As late as the 1950s Puerto Ricans faced a problem of shifting identities with regard to both ethnicity and race. On ethnicity, "In New York the terms 'Hispano' and 'Latino' have been substituted for that of 'Puerto Rican', because the latter, in more ways than one, has become 'bad public relations' identification for New York Puerto Ricans. It is associated with unfavorable pictures of the behavior and respectability of Puerto Ricans, which are not necessarily true or real. Even when used in Spanish and by Puerto Ricans themselves, it may convey an assumption of undesirable characteristics of the person referred to." On race, the darker members of the group "continue to associate with and identify with Puerto Ricans as they do not desire to be identified with American Negroes."

Probably the key factor inhibiting Puerto Rican assimilation is color. Some unknown percentage of the population is discernably nonwhite. Glazer and Moynihan, among others, have compared Puerto Ricans and the Italian immigrants who came to the country at the turn of the century, speculating on the likelihood of a similar adaptation process for Puerto Ricans. The complicating factor is color. The Italians were white and some portion of the Puerto Rican population is not.

Puerto Rican attitudes towards color have been more complicated and less vicious than those of Anglos and this has made their adaptation more difficult. From the Puerto Rican perspective mainland attitudes on race are simple-minded and malevolent. The Puerto Rican lexicon on color is much richer than that found on the mainland. An individual regarded as a "Negro" by an Anglo might be termed triguero, indio, grifo, Hispano, or Negro by a Puerto Rican. An individual designated "white" by an Anglo might be referred to as Hispano, grifo, Triguero Hispano, or white by a Puerto Rican. The terminology reflects very fine discriminations in terms of skin color, physiognomy, and hair texture. On the level of interaction "As in the United States . . . . two major racial groups are recognized socially; they are white and Negro. But the recognition of these two groups does not result in the formation of two distinct subgroups of caste-like separation as it does in the United States . . . . Much social interaction takes place and many interpersonal relations of an intimate and warm nature occur among individuals regardless of whether or not they have Negro ancestry and whether they look Negroid or white, though there is a stated preference for being white."

Color differences among Puerto Ricans sometimes cut across families, complicating the process of bifurcation of the Puerto Rican community into a mobile, white group and a nonmobile, black group. Language is another barrier to assimilation and a cause of discrimination. More conventional discrimination by trade unions and landlords has also served to lock Puerto Ricans into low-paying jobs and restrict them to decaying sections of the city.

Puerto Rican Power

The black power movement seems to have set off an upheaval among the numerous outcast and outsider groups in the United States. In the wake of that movement has come the "red power" and "brown power" movements (both discussed in this book), the Womens' Liberation Movement, the Gay Liberation movement, and not unsurprisingly, a rennaissance movement among Puerto Ricans. The fundamental process at work seems to have been the development among the nation's variously oppressed groups of the belief that if the most oppressed among them could rise up, then all might follow suit.

In mobilizing themselves Puerto Ricans had to face the fundamental issue of color differences within the group. As indicated, some segment of the Puerto Rican population is discernably nonwhite. A number of observers have indicated that light-skinned Puerto Ricans attempt to move into the mainstream and lose themselves while darker-skinned Puerto Ricans sought to differentiate themselves from blacks by, among other things, speaking Spanish in public.

It is not at all clear how Puerto Ricans have resolved this problem; there have been a number of instances, however, of common action by blacks and Puerto Ricans. Specifically, a black and Puerto Rican student coalition in Newark, New Jersey has addressed itself to the task of translating the numerical majority of blacks and Puerto Ricans in the city into control of the machinery of city government. Blacks and Puerto Ricans united at City College of New York during the academic year 1968-1969 to push a common set of demands, among them the requiring of Spanish on the part of students preparing to teach in the city's heavily Puerto Rican school system.

The Puerto Rican movement on the mainland is addressed to many of the same issues that agitate blacks: poor schools, bad housing, widespread poverty. Their programmatic responses like those of blacks, browns, and reds has been control over the institutions affecting Puerto Rican community and the passage of legislation dealing in various ways with problems of deprivation.

On the island an independence movement continues to be active. Most observers do not take it seriously, but it may yet be heard from.

New York City politics are fundamentally more complicated than those of other cities. It is difficult to achieve tangible victories and in the welter of events which assault the senses of the New Yorker it is difficult to gain the attention of the public long enough to enjoy even a symbolic victory. The city is like a stage crowded with different players, each acting out a part in a different play—clowns turn their tumbles over the huddled forms of old women who never cease weeping, prophets thunder to catonic crowds, one walks past bums, their eyes turned inward on some endless movie playing in the dark of their minds.

Blacks and other minority groups can talk reasonably about coming to power in other cities. In New York, the complex structure of city government, the tangled articulation of institutions and people, defeats any attempt to discover where power resides. On a certain level, becoming involved in politics means joining the various democratic party clubs. The clubs function mainly to divide spoils and to make faithful party men available for office. Access to power via the clubhouse route is a time-consuming process which does not necessarily translate itself into meaningful control of the resources necessary for dealing in a significant way with community deprivation. Harlem has had representation at the state and congressional level for decades.

Institutional politics among Puerto Ricans is embodied mostly in the figure of Herman Badillo, formerly Borough president of the Bronx; noninstitutional politics by the Young Lords, a group of young men, impressed by the efforts of the Black Panthers to organize such things as breakfast programs for hungry children in the ghetto.

Puerto Ricans maintain closer ties to the island than Mexican Americans do to Mexico. There is a good deal of travel back and forth and extended families span both places. This essay has briefly sketched in the New York portion of the picture. The articles in this section provide brilliant descriptions of life styles on the island, descriptions which are necessary to any understanding of Puerto Ricans on the mainland. In a sense there is only one Puerto Rican community. This essay and the articles have dealt with that community as a whole.

FURTHER READING

Island in the City by Dan Wakefield (New York: Corinth Books, Inc., 1957) is a journalistic account of life in Spanish Harlem, but probably dated now.
Spanish Harlem by Patricia Sexton (New York: Harper Colophon Books, 1965) is a very good study by a very good sociologist.
Up From Puerto Rico by Elena Padilla (New York: Columbia University Press, 1959) is a good ethnographic study of the Puerto Rican community in New York.

La Vida by Oscar Lewis (New York: Random House, 1966) is a standard work on Puerto Rican life styles in Puerto Rico and New York City.

Down These Mean Streets by Piri Thomas (New York: Alfred A. Knopf, 1967) is the Puerto Rican equivalent of *Manchild in the Promised Land.*

Spanish-Speaking Groups in the United States by John H. Burma (Duke University Press, 1954) contains a chapter on Puerto Ricans, good for its time but probably dated now.

Beyond the Melting Pot by Nathan Glazer and Daniel P. Moynihan (Cambridge, Mass.: The M.I.T. Press, 1963) has a comprehensive chapter on Puerto Ricans and an excellent comparative study of New York City's ethnic communities.

"The Puerto Rican in New York City" by Warren Brown, *Race Prejudice and Discrimination* (New York: Alfred A. Knopf, 1951) good in terms of how the Puerto Rican community looked to a social scientist two decades ago.

Brothers Under the Skin by Carey McWilliams (Boston: Little, Brown and Company, 1942) is a heavy rap by an old-time radical.

"The Adjustment of Puerto Ricans to New York City" by Joseph P. Fitzpatrick, in *Minority Problems,* edited by Arnold M. Rose and Caroline B. Rose (New York: Harper and Row, 1965) touches the high points in terms of the characteristics of Puerto Ricans in New York.

Even the Saints Cry

OSCAR LEWIS

"You cannot take people out of an old-fashioned slum, where reality has been giving them a grim, distorted education for years, place them in a project, and expect them to exhibit all kinds of gentle, middle-class virtues."

Michael Harrington

This article describes the experiences of a young Puerto Rican mother, Cruz Rios, who moved from La Esmeralda—one of the oldest slums in San Juan only a short distance from the governor's palace—about four miles east to Villa Hermosa, a new government housing project in a middle-class section of Rio Piedras. Cruz' story illustrates the difficult problems of adjustment in her new environment and helps us understand why, in spite of the efforts of well-intentioned governments and the spending of huge sums of money on public housing, the positive effects hoped for by social planners are not always forthcoming.

135

When I began my study of Cruz in 1963, she was just 17 and living alone on relief with her two children. She lived in a small, dark, one-room apartment for which she paid a rental of eight dollars a month. Her kitchen was a tiny corner alcove equipped with a three-burner kerosene stove and a water faucet jutting out from the wall. She shared a run-down hall toilet with two other families and paid a neighbor $1.50 a month for the privilege of an extension cord which supplied her with electricity.

Cruz, a crippled, mulatto girl with reddish brown kinky hair and a pretty face, was lame since early childhood. She left school after the fifth grade, set up house with her sweetheart at 14 and gave birth to her first child at 15. Two years later, before the birth of her second child, she separated from her husband, Emilio, who refused to recognize the baby as his own.

Part I gives the reader a glimpse of living conditions in the slum; part II, recorded five months after Cruz had moved, gives her reactions to the housing project. (Names of all places and people in this tape-recorded narrative have been changed to guarantee the anonymity of the narrator.)

I: Conditions in the Slum

Here in La Esmeralda, the only thing that disturbs me are the rats. Lice, bedbugs, and rats have always been a problem in my room. When I moved in here a year ago, the first thing I found were little baby rats. "Kill them!" my friend Gloria said. *"Ay Bendito!* I can't do it. Poor little things—they look like children," I said, and I left them there in a hole. The next day they were gone. I didn't kill them, they just disappeared. I cleaned up the house and about a month later they were going back and forth through the room from one hole to another, with me just looking at them.

When Alejandro was living with me, more rats came because there was a hen with eggs under the house. A rat had given birth and had eaten some of the chicks. The owner took the hen and 29 chicks out of there because there were baby rats underneath the hen too. The man threw them out but a week later they came back and were all over the place, even getting into the pan with the baby's milk and eating up whatever I left around.

One Sunday my *mamá* said, "Let's buy a rat trap and see if we can't get rid of some of them." Well, we tried it and that day between us and the next-door neighbor we caught 29 little rats. After a while, more came. Anita used to chase them across the room to see if she could catch them, and the boys who came to the house would say, "Look, a rat."

I would tell them, "Let it be, it's one of the family. They keep me company, now that I'm all by myself. I'm raising them for soup."

So I left them alone, but before I knew it, there were great big rats here. One Sunday I said to Catín, who had just eaten a breaded cutlet, "Catín, you'd better go bathe or the rats will eat you up." Then I forgot about it and she lay down. Later I took a bath and went to bed. About midnight, Catín screamed, *"Ay, ay, ay, it bit me!"* The first thing that came to my mind was that it was a snake or a scorpion. "What bit you?" I asked and when I turned on the light, she said, "Look, look!" and I could see a rat running away.

She had been bitten on the arm and I could see the little teeth marks. I squeezed out the blood and smeared urine and bay rum on it.

Then I said, "Catín, you'd better come into my bed with me. God knows whether it was because the crib is dirty or you are dirty." I was wearing only panties, Chuito and Anita were naked, but Catín was wearing a jacket and pants. Well, later that same rat came and bit her again on the other arm. I sprinkled bay rum all over the bed where she was sleeping and rubbed it on her and nothing else happened that night.

The next day I went to the church and told the Sister that the girl had been bitten by a rat. She told me that if Catín didn't start running a fever, to leave her alone, and if she did, to take her to the hospital. Then I said to Catín, "You see? That's what happens when you don't bathe." She took a bath every day after that.

At the end of the year, Anita got a rat bite on the lip. I squeezed it out for her and it dried up and she didn't get a fever or anything. A few days after that, I was sitting in a chair with my arm hanging down when a rat came and *pra!* it tried to take off my finger. It wanted human flesh. I lifted my hand, and the rat ran to a hole and disappeared.

Then I said to myself, "These rats have to be finished off. I can't live like this with so many blessed rats. There are more rats than people." And I bought a trap from the man next door. I fixed the bacon myself and put it in the trap. First I caught a real big rat, then another, and another. Three in all that same night. But there were still more left.

The next morning, I heard screams coming from Rosa Maria's room up above. I said, "Rosa, what's wrong?" Her little boy was crying and shaking his hand, with a rat hanging from it. "Kill it," I said, but he answered, "I can't. Its teeth are stuck in my finger." Finally he got if off by dragging it along the floor. Rosa Maria attended him but the next day the child had a fever which kept going up. The doctor said that the boy was getting tetanus and had to go to the hospital.

The people upstairs leave a lot of rotting clothes piled there, and cans of food and rice. If they don't get rid of that filth, the rats won't leave. I asked the landlord to cover the holes because the rats keep coming in and out as if they were in a bus terminal. He said he didn't live here and I should do it myself.

There are lots of cockroaches in my room too. And new fleas have come in, I don't know from where, except probably from the rats themselves. There are also crickets and lizards. These houses are hollow underneath, and below the floor there's a lot of old boards and filth and all kinds of garbage that has accumulated, and at night the animals come crawling up.

I've noticed that it's on Thursday nights that the rats give us the most trouble. Every other Thursday, before the social worker comes, I clean my house from top to bottom so there are no crumbs on the floor for the rats to eat and no dirty dishes for them to clean. I've learned that unless I leave something for them, the rats come closer and closer to us. When the house is clean, we are in more danger of getting bitten.

II: Reactions to the Project

The social worker told me it would be a good idea to get the children out of La Esmeralda because there's so much delinquency there. My moving to the housing project was practically her idea; she insisted and insisted. Finally one day she came to me and said, "Tomorrow you have to move to the *caserío* in Villa Hermosa." I didn't want to upset her because she's been good to me, so I said okay.

You should have seen this place when I moved in. It

was bursting with garbage and smelling of shit, pure shit. Imagine, when the social worker opened the door that first day, a breeze happened to blow her way. She stepped back and said, "Wait, I can't go in. This is barbarous." I had to go outside with her. I tell you, the people who lived here before me were dirtier than the dirtiest pig. When I moved out of my little room in La Esmeralda, I scrubbed it so clean you could have eaten off the floor. Whoever moved in could see that a decent person had lived there. And then I came here and found this pig-sty, and the place looked so big I felt too little and weak to get it clean. So, fool that I am, instead of sending out for a mop and getting right down to work, I just stood in a corner and cried. I locked the door and stayed in all day, weeping. I cried floods.

And this place isn't like La Esmeralda, you know, where there's so much liveliness and noise and something is always going on. Here you never see any movement on the street, not one little domino or card game or anything. The place is dead. People act as if they're angry or in mourning. Either they don't know how to live or they're afraid to. And yet it's full of shameless good-for-nothings. It's true what the proverb says, "May God deliver me from quiet places; I can defend myself in the wild ones."

Everything was so strange to me when I first moved here that I was scared to death. I hated to go out because it's hard to find your way back to this place even if you know the address. The first couple of times I got lost, and I didn't dare ask anybody the way for fear they would fall on me and beat me. If anyone knocked on my door I thought four times before deciding to open it. Then when I did, I took a knife along. But I'm not like that any more. I've made my decision: if someone wants to kill me, let him. I can't live shut in like that. And if anybody interferes with me it will be the worse for them. I have a couple of tricks up my sleeve and can really fuck things up for anybody when I want to.

After a few days, I finally started cleaning up the place. I scrubbed the floors and put everything in order. I even painted the whole apartment, although I had to fight tooth and nail with the man in charge of the buildings in order to get the paint. That old man wanted to get something from me in return, but I wouldn't give it to him. I never have been attracted to old men.

The apartment is a good one. I have a living room, bedroom, kitchen, porch and my own private bathroom. That's something I never had in La Esmeralda. I clean it every morning and when the children use it I go and pull the chain right away.

I never had a kitchen sink in La Esmeralda either, and here I have a brand new one. It's easy to wash the dishes in these double sinks because they're so wide and comfortable. The only trouble is the water, because sometimes it goes off and the electricity, too—three times since I've been here.

I still don't have an ice-box or refrigerator but the stove here is the first electric one I've ever had in my life. I didn't know how to light it the day I moved in. I tried everything I could think of, backward and forward. Luckily, the social worker came and she lit it for me, but even so I didn't learn and Nanda had to show me again that afternoon. She has worked for rich people so long that she knows all those things. I really miss my own little kerosene stove, but Nanda wanted it, so what could I do? She's my *mamá* and if she hankered after a star I would climb up to heaven to get it for her if I could.

The main advantage of the electric stove is that when I have a lot of work to do and it gets to be ten or eleven o'clock, I just connect the stove and have lunch ready in no time. In La Esmeralda I had to wait for the kerosene to light up well before I could even start to cook. And this stove doesn't smoke and leave soot all over the place, either. Still, if the power fails again or is cut off because I don't pay my bill, the kids will just have to go hungry. I won't even be able to heat a cup of milk for them. In La Esmeralda, whenever I didn't have a quarter to buy a full gallon of kerosene, I got ten cents worth. But who's going to sell you five or ten cents worth of electricity?

I haven't seen any rats here, just one tiny little mouse. It doesn't bother me much because it lives down below, in a hole at the bottom of the stairs. There's no lack of company anywhere, I guess—rats in La Esmeralda and lots of little cockroaches here.

This apartment is so big that I don't have to knock myself out keeping it in order. There's plenty of room for my junk. I even have closets here, and lots of shelves. I have so many shelves and so few dishes that I have to put a dish here and a dish there just to keep each shelf from being completely empty. All the counters and things are no use at all to me, because I just cook a bit of oatmeal for the children and let them sit anywhere to eat it since I have no dishes with which to set a table. Half of my plates broke on the way from La Esmeralda. I guess they wanted to stay back there where they weren't so lonely.

Here even my saints cry! They look so sad. They think I am punishing them. This house is so big I had to separate the saints and hang them up in different places just to cover the empty walls. In La Esmeralda I kept them all together to form a little altar, and I lit candles for them.

In La Esmeralda they helped me, but here I ask until I'm tired of asking and they don't help me at all. They are punishing me.

In La Esmeralda I never seemed to need as many things as here. I think it is because we all had about the same, so we didn't need any more. But here, when you go to other people's apartment and see all their things . . . It's not that I'm jealous. God forbid! I don't want anyone to have less than they have. It's only that I would like to have things of my own too.

What does bother me is the way people here come into my apartment and furnish the place with their mouths. They start saying, "Oh, here's where the set of furniture should go; you need a TV set in that corner and this one is just right for a record-player." And so on. I bite my tongue to keep from swearing at them because, damn it, I have good taste too. I know a TV set would look fine in that corner, but if I don't have the money to buy one, how can I put it there? That's what I like about La Esmeralda—if people there could help someone, they did; if not, they kept their mouths shut.

I really would like a TV though, because they don't have public sets here, the way they do in La Esmeralda. I filled in some blanks for that program, Queen for a Day, to see if I can get one as a gift. It was Nanda's idea and she's so lucky that maybe I will get it. If I do, then at least I could spend the holidays looking at TV. And the children might stay home instead of wandering around the neighborhood so much.

The traffic here really scares me. That's the main reason I don't like this place. Cars scud by like clouds in a high wind and, I'm telling you, I'm always afraid a car will hit the children. If something should happen to my little penguins, I'd go mad, I swear I would. My kids are little devils, and when I bring them in through the front door, they slip out again by climbing over the porch railing. Back in La Esmeralda, where our house was so small, they had to play out in the street whenever people came over, but here there is plenty of room to run around indoors.

Maybe I was better off in La Esmeralda. You certainly have to pay for the comforts you have here! Listen, I'm jittery, really nervous, because if you fail to pay the rent even once here, the following month you're thrown out. I hardly ever got behind on my payments in La Esmeralda, but if I did, I knew that they wouldn't put me out on the street. It's true that my rent is only $6.50 a month here while I paid $11.50 in La Esmeralda, but there I didn't have a water bill and I paid only $1.50 a month for electricity. Here I have already had to pay $3.50 for electricity and if I use more than the minimum they allow in water, I'll have to pay for that too. And I do so much washing!

It's a fact that as long as I lived in La Esmeralda I could always scare up some money, but here I'm always broke. I've gone as much as two days without eating. I don't play the races at El Comandante any more. I can't afford to. And I can't sell *bolita* numbers here because several cops live in this *caserío* and the place is full of detectives. Only the other day I almost sold a number to one of them, but luckily I was warned in time. I don't want to be arrested for anything in the world, not because I'm scared of being in jail but because of the children.

Since I can't sell numbers here, I sell Avon cosmetics. I like the pretty sets of china they give away, and I'm trying to sell a lot so that they'll give me one. But there's hardly any profit in it for me.

In La Esmeralda I could get an old man now and then to give me five dollars for sleeping with him. But here I haven't found anything like that at all. The truth is, if a man comes here and tries to strike up a conversation I usually slam the door in his face. So, well, I have this beautiful, clean apartment, but what good does it do me? Where am I to get money? I can't dig for it.

In La Esmeralda we used to buy things cheap from thieves. They stole from people who lived far away and then they came to La Esmeralda through one of the side entrances to sell. And who the hell is going to go looking for his things down there? Not a chance! You hardly ever saw a rich person in La Esmeralda. We didn't like them, and we scared them off. But so far as I can tell, these dopes around here always steal from the *blanquitos,* the rich people, nearby. Suppose one of them took it into his head to come here to look for the missing stuff? What then?

Since I've moved I'm worse off than I have ever been before, because now I realize all the things I lack and, besides, the rich people around here are always wanting everything for themselves. In La Esmeralda you can bum a nickel from anyone. But with these people, the more they have, the more they want. It's everything for themselves. If you ask them for work, they'll find something for you to do fast enough, but when it's time to pay you'd think it hurt them to pull a dollar out of their pocket.

Listen, to get a few beans from some people who live in a house near here I had to help pick and shell them. People here are real hard and stingy. What's worse, they take advantage of you. The other day I ironed all day long for a woman and all I got for it was two dollars and my dinner. I felt like throwing the money in her face but I just calmly took it. I would have been paid six dollars at the very least for a whole day's ironing in La Esmeralda. At another lady's house near here I cooked, washed the dishes, even scrubbed the floor, and for all that she just gave me one of her old dresses, which I can't even wear because it's too big for me.

Right now, I don't have a cent. The lady next door lets me charge the food for breakfast at her husband's *kiosko*. She's become so fond of me, you can't imagine. Her husband won't sell on credit to anybody, but there's nothing impossible for the person who is really interested in helping you out. She trusts me, so she lets me write down what I take and keep the account myself.

I buy most of my food at the Villa Hermosa grocery. It's a long way from here and I have to walk it on foot every time I need something, like rice or tomato sauce. It's a supermarket, so they don't give credit, but everything is cheaper there, much cheaper. A can of tomato sauce costs seven cents there and 10 cents in La Esmeralda. Ten pounds of rice costs $1.25 in La Esmeralda and 99 cents here. The small bottles of King Pine that cost 15 cents each in La Esmeralda are two for a quarter here.

Sometimes Public Welfare gives me food, but not always, and I don't like most of the things they give. That long-grained rice doesn't taste like anything. It's like eating hay. The meat they give has fat on top and it comes in a can and it's real dark. They say it's corned beef but I don't know. The same goes for that powdered milk. Who could drink the stuff? In La Esmeralda I saved it until I was really hard up and then I sold it to anybody who was willing to shell out a quarter for it to feed it to their animals or something. But I don't dare do that here because it's federal government food, and it's against the law to sell it. I could get into trouble that way in a place like this, where I don't know anybody. I might try to sell that stuff to a detective without realizing who he was and I'd land in jail.

I haven't been to La Esmeralda often since I moved here, because I can't afford it. Every trip costs 40 cents, 20 cents each way. I want to pay off all my debts in La Esmeralda so that I can hold my head high and proud when I go there. I want people to think I've bettered myself because one can't be screwed all one's life. Even now when I visit, still owing money as I do, I put on my best clothes and always try to carry a little cash. I do this so Minerva, Emilio's aunt, won't get the idea I'm starving or anything like that. She really suffers when she sees me in La Esmeralda, and I do all that just to bother her. I dress up the kids real nice and take them to call on everybody except her.

When I first moved out of La Esmeralda, nobody knew that I was leaving, in the first place because it made me sad and in the second place because that old Minerva had gone around telling everybody she hoped I'd clear out. She even said it to my face. I'd yell back at her, "What right do you have to say that? Did you buy La Esmeralda or something?"

Another reason why I hardly ever go to La Esmeralda is because Emilio spies on me. He has come after me in the *caserío* just the way he did in La Esmeralda, though not as often. He likes to use the shower in my new apartment when he comes. When I start home after visiting La Esmeralda, he gets into his car and drives along behind me, offering to give me a lift. But, listen, I wouldn't get into that car even if I had to walk all the way from San Juan to Villa Hermosa. I put a curse on that car, such a tremendous curse that I'm just waiting to see it strike. I did it one day when Anita had asthma and I had no money to take her to the hospital. I happened to glance out of the window and I saw Emilio stretched out in his car, relaxed as could be, as if he deserved nothing but the best. I let go and yelled with all the breath in my chest, "I hope to God someday you'll wear that car as a hat. I hope it turns to dust with you all fucked up inside it." Now I can't ride in the car, because I'm afraid the curse will come true some time when both of us are in it.

You can't imagine how lonely I feel here. I have friends, but they're sort of artificial, pasted-on friends. I couldn't confide. in them at all. For example, I got pregnant a little while ago, and I had to have an abortion. I nearly went crazy thinking about it. Having a baby is nothing, it's the burden you have to take on afterwards, especially with a cowardly husband like mine who takes the easiest way out, denying that the child is his. So there I was, pregnant and, you know, I was ashamed. I was already out of La Esmeralda, see? Well, I know that my womb is weak, so I took two doses of Epsom salts with quinine and out came the kid. You can't imagine how unpleasant that is. In La Esmeralda you can tell everybody about it, and that sort of eases your heart. But here I didn't tell anybody. These girls I know here are *señoritas,* mere children, and something like that . . . *ay, bendito!*

But, to tell you the truth, I don't know what they call a *señorita* here in Villa Hermosa. The way it is in La Esmeralda, a girl and boy fall in love. For a few months they control themselves. Then they can't any more, and the boy does what he has to do to the girl. The hole is bigger than the full moon and that's that. They tell everybody and become husband and wife in the eyes of all the world. There's no trying to hide it. But here you see girls, who by rights should already have had a couple of kids, trying to keep from being found out. They'll go to a hotel with their sweethearts and let them stick their pricks into every hole in their body except the right one. And then they're so brazen as to come out of that hotel claiming they're still *señoritas*. It's plain shameless.

There are some policemen here who make love like this to some girls I know. Well, the policeman who did it to my friend Mimi came and told me that if I loaned him my bed for a little while he would give me three pesos. As that money wouldn't be bad at all and as he wasn't going to do it to me, I rented him the bed and grabbed the three pesos. Let them go screw! They locked themselves in the bedroom for a little while and then they went away. It was none of my business. If they didn't do it here, they would go do it somewhere else. And she didn't lose her virginity or anything here. So my hands are clean.

Sometimes I want to go back to La Esmeralda to live and other times I don't. It's not that I miss my family so much. On the contrary, relatives can be very bothersome. But you do need them in case you get sick because then you can dump the children on them. Sometimes I cry for loneliness here. Sometimes I'm bored to death. There's more neighborliness in La Esmeralda. I was used to having good friends stop by my house all the time. I haven't seen much of this neighborhood because I never go out. There's a Catholic church nearby but I've never been there. And I haven't been to the movies once since I've been living here. In La Esmeralda I used to go now and then. And in La Esmeralda, when nothing else was going on, you could at least hear the sea.

In La Esmeralda nobody ever made fun of my lameness. On the contrary, it was an advantage because everyone went out of his way to help me: "Let me help the lame girl. Let me buy *bolita* numbers from Lame Crucita, because cripples bring luck." But it isn't like that here, where people just laugh. That's why I'd like to live in La Esmeralda again or have Nanda move in here with me.

The social worker told me that I could go to the hospital and have an operation to fix my back. But who could I leave my little baby crows with? And suppose what they do is take my guts out in order to make me look right? Still, now that I live in a place like Villa Hermosa, I would like to have an operation to make me straight.

November 1966

The Puerto Rican
Independence Movement

ARTHUR LIEBMAN

"Yanqui go home," the demonstrators chant as they parade down the major thoroughfares. Nationalists tear down American flags and fly their own banners. The major university is in political ferment. Student radicals continuously denounce the United States. Bombs explode in American owned or controlled stores and businesses, as well as in luxurious tourist hotels. A radio station is seized and a broadcast appeals for revolution against Yankee imperialism. The scenario is familiar.

One aspect, however, distinguishes it. These demonstrators, these student radicals and these planters of bombs who want the Americans out are themselves American citizens. They are Puerto Ricans. For the moment they are only a small proportion of the Puerto Rican populace, but their numbers are growing.

In the past two years Puerto Rican nationalists have set off bombs in more than 100 stores, businesses and hotels, causing more than $15 million in destruction of property and lost sales or patronage. Bargain Town, Sears and Woolworth's have been among the businesses bombed. line at Ramey Air Force Base.

Students at the University of Puerto Rico (UPR), who prior to 1964 had not been involved in any political disturbance for almost 20 years, have in the last two helped keep the University in a continual state of political turmoil. Militant *independentistas* or supporters of independence have been the principal catalysts. Their numbers and influence have increased appreciably in recent years not only at the UPR but within the high schools as well. This October, in their boldest act to date, student militants burned and ransacked the ROTC building on the UPR campus.

In the last two years, pro-independence groups outside the university have organized demonstrations and rallies in which crowds estimated at 10,000 to 20,000 persons have participated—figures considered impressive for an island of less than three million people. Although these have been peaceful assemblies, the impassioned pro-independence and anti-American oratory has reflected the feelings of many of the participants. Their response has been enthusiastic.

It is puzzling to many Americans to discover such strong animosity toward their country among a people who have seemingly so richly benefited from their association with the United States. When Puerto Rico was acquired from Spain as war booty in 1898, the island was a virtually resourceless and impoverished land suffering from years of long neglect. Today, by any economic or social indicator, Puerto Rico can be considered an advanced country. It has a per capita income of $1,100, which is higher than that of any country in Latin America. Eighty-five percent of its children attend school; Puerto Rico ranks fourth in the world with respect to proportion of its college age cohort enrolled in institutions of higher education, 19 percent. Infant mortality is low, the lowest in Latin America, while life expectancy is 70 years, similar to that of the United States. There is a television set in almost every house and the per capita distribution of automobiles and trucks rivals that of the mainland. Currently, Puerto Rico has one of the world's fastest rates of economic growth. There can be little doubt that this island's social and economic conditions are attributable to Puerto Rico's ties with the United States. Who, then, wants to sever forcefully the golden chain which binds the Puerto Rican Commonwealth to its American benefactor? And, why?

There are several political organizations committed to independence for Puerto Rico. Among the most militant, active and vocal are the Pro-Independence Movement (*Movimiento Pro-Independence,* MPI) and the Federation of Pro-Independence University Students (*Federacion de Universitarios Pro-Independencia,* FUPI). More violent than the MPI or FUPI is the clandestine Commandos for Armed Liberation (CAL), the group that plants the bombs. The least militant of the pro-independence organizations is the Puerto Rican Independence Party (*Partido Independentista Puertorriqueno,* PIP).

The MPI and FUPI consider the Puerto Rican government to be illegitimate, a colonial puppet of the United States. Neither will participate in any election or governmental body because it might lend legitimacy to the Puerto Rican government. Consequently, at election time both center their efforts on voter boycott campaigns. The strident tone of these groups is a measure of the mounting intensity of feeling about independence, as is the increasing use of Marxist-Leninist rhetoric and declarations of solidarity with the Vietcong and Fidel Castro. Even the PIP, noted for its concern with legality and respectability, has begun to sound (and act) somewhat more militant and impatient on the subject of independence than it has in years past. In 1967, the PIP boycotted the official plebiscite and recently its leaders have shared public platforms with their counterparts from the MPI, both acts which would have been uncharacteristic of the PIP a few years ago.

Much of the impact that the pro-independence militant organizations have been able to make stems from the nature of their memberships. The activist core of the MPI consists of youthful intellectuals, academicians and independent professionals. Members of FUPI are recruited from among the brightest university students; sociological study as well as unsympathetic University of Puerto Rico officials have attested to this. Both memberships are dedicated to the cause of independence and individuals often subordinate their careers to the demands of their organizations. They work hard and long hours, manning picket lines, mounting demonstrations, passing out leaflets and attending countless meetings. Both the MPI and FUPI have gifted and articulate leaders. And each of these groups has been able to attract considerable attention from the island's media.

Nevertheless, while both the MPI and FUPI are growing in size, they are still small organizations. And despite the increase in pro-independence militancy, the adherents of independence, moderate or militant, do not represent a majority of the Puerto Rican population. In fact, numerical support for statehood appears to be greater than that for independence. In the 1968 gubernatorial election, the statehood candidate, Louis A. Ferre, won with 43 percent of the votes, a figure sufficient for victory due to a split within the long governing Popular Democratic Party (*Partido Popular Democratico*, PPD). In every gubernatorial election since 1952, when it garnered 13 percent of the ballots, the statehood party has increased its percentage of the vote, reaching its peak in the 1968 election. This is in contrast to the PIP whose share of the votes has remained at 3 percent over the last three elections.

It should be stressed, however, that the magnitude and intensity of support for independence, particularly that type espoused by militants, are not reflected in ballot counts. On the one hand, the split among *independentista* organizations with respect to participation in elections means that the vote obtained by the PIP represents only a fraction of the independence supporters and these are in all likelihood the moderates. On the other hand, there are too many cases in history in which there were discrepancies between the electoral strength and the social power of radical groups to simply permit the number and distribution of votes to be the final arbiter of the strength of a political organization. In the United States most observers would agree that there has been an upsurge in black militancy in the last few years. However, according to Gary T. Marx of Harvard, this fact has neither been reflected in public opinion polls nor in local elections. The number of violent acts, the size and nature of demonstrations, the attitude of intellectuals and the responses of governmental authorities must be looked to, along with election returns, as indicators of group strength or social change. Also, there is nothing to prevent the rise of two opposing tendencies—in this case, the support for statehood and the support for independence—each of which may use different political mechanisms for its purposes.

But why the rise in pro-independence militancy at this

particular juncture of Puerto Rican history? The political status of the island has long been the most important and most divisive issue in Puerto Rican politics, *except for the last quarter of a century.* Beginning in 1940 when he led his PPD to victory, Muñoz Marin, the ex-governor and leader of the Popular Democratic Party has been able through the force of his personality, his political genius, and party apparatus to mute the debate and overt concern over the status issue. The policy and basic program to which he and his party have generally adhered since the founding of the PPD in 1938 has been to subordinate the status issue to that of social and economic reform. In the late 1940s and early 1950s Muñoz formulated and promoted the Commonwealth solution which became a reality in 1952. Originally he envisioned Commonwealth as a temporary solution, one that would combine the positive aspects of both statehood and independence and afford Puerto Rico the opportunity to develop economically while forestalling an acrimonious debate over the status issue. By 1965, however, he became convinced that Commonwealth was not a temporary stop-gap but a *permanent* solution. Either statehood or independence, Muñoz felt, would be too costly to the Puerto Rican economy.

By the mid-1960s, Muñoz and the PPD became unable to effectively restrain the debate and the political struggle over the island's status. It is simply not possible to avoid indefinitely the most basic political issue in a society. Muñoz grew older, stepped down from the governorship and was no longer able to impose his will upon his countrymen or significant sections of his own party. The middle class, which was spawned by his economic policies, turned from the PPD to the support of the statehood party. Applying the lesson they had learned from Muñoz, the bourgeoisie felt that its economic position could be better protected under statehood than under autonomy. At the same time, however, intellectuals and idealistic youth seriously began to question if the Commonwealth position was needed any longer to buy time for Puerto Rico. The plebiscite of 1967, the election campaign and the victory of a pro-statehood governor in 1968 signified the end of the moratorium on the status issue.

These events also signified the end of a consensus that had been erected over a period of 25 years by Muñoz Marin. The demise of support for the Commonwealth position has contributed to the raise of militancy in Puerto Rico. Instead of three positions on the status issue there soon will be two, which means that the island will be divided into two opposing political camps on an issue that both sides consider to be important. Increasingly the news from Puerto Rico indicates the extent of the cleavage taking place. Muñoz Marin, the moderate architect of consensus, has recently denounced Governor Ferre for his assimilationist policies and has urged the Puerto Rican people to "defend their cultural heritage." A prominent journalist for *El Mundo,* a paper unsympathetic to FUPI and MPI, has called for an unrestricted battle against Governor Ferre and his New Progressive party. He complains of being forced to choose sides. "The trouble is as soon as you say you're Puerto Rican someone from the New Progressive Party jumps up and calls you anti-American or even Communist." And even more recently the Chancellor of the UPR, Abraham Diaz Gonzalez, a man not noted for his political activity, was forced from his post, reportedly because he surrounded himself with pro-independence aides and was soft on FUPI. What seems to be occurring in Puerto Rico is the cumulative radicalization of pro-independence sympathizers and supporters. The upsurge of militance and violence by elements within the pro-independence forces is the logical culmination of this process.

Other factors have also aided the rise of militancy in Puerto Rico. A very significant one involves identity and self-hatred. Both under Spain and the United States, Puerto Ricans have been subject to conditions that inhibited the healthy growth of a positive sense of identity. The social, economic and cultural institutions that helped forge meaningful identities among other national groups were weak or absent in Puerto Rico. Prior to 1898, the upper strata, who are generally the expressive carriers of a cultural tradition, were Spanish or preferred to consider themselves as such. Because of the mercantilistic policies of Spain, the middle strata were few in number and they, too, looked to Spain rather than their own people for their sense of meaning. The poor transportation facilities and the diffuse residence patterns of the lower strata, most of whom lived in the countryside, restricted the opportunity of those people to mingle with other Puerto Ricans outside of their local area. This limited the development of a national sense. The Church was staffed by Spaniards and was oriented to Spain. There were few schools at any level and no university. The rich sent their children to Spain for higher education. In short, as Glazer and Moynihan have commented, Puerto Rico was defective with respect to ". . . the net of culture which keeps up pride and encourages effort." Indicative of this weak sense of national identity and pride is the fact that unlike the other Latin American colonies of Spain, Puerto Rico never fought for its independence except for a two-day skirmish at Lares in 1868.

The situation did not noticeably improve after 1898 when the Americans replaced the Spanish. An educational system was developed and a university built along an American model. The policy of American educators appeared to be aimed at reducing if not eliminating the Hispanic or Puerto Rican identity of the school children. In 1898, for example, Americans established English as the sole language of instruction at all grade levels despite the shortage of teachers who could speak the language. The Puerto Rican educational system continues to be oriented toward the United States even though Puerto Ricans now control it. Many Puerto Rican teachers and administrators go to the mainland for training. A large proportion of the texts are written by mainlanders. And, of course, the academic accreditation bodies which evaluate the Puerto Rican schools are American.

The generation coming of age in Puerto Rico today has learned little of Puerto Rican history. Elementary schools did not teach the subject and the high schools usually taught only a one semester course. Students in the Schools of Humanities, Social Sciences and Education do receive a semblance of systematic exposure to Puerto Rican history; but in all likelihood Puerto Ricans in the public schools of New York City learn more about their heritage than those on the island. In the private schools on the island, where growing numbers of middle- and upper-class parents are sending their children, the American orientation is pronounced; English remains the language of instruction in these schools.

The American influence in the cultural sphere extends beyond the formal educational system. The mass media are predominately American in orientation and content. Television and movie screens are filled with American shows and movies. The news of the outside world is transmitted to Puerto Rico via the American wire services, the three

American networks, Miami newspapers and the *New York Times*. News and contact with Latin American affairs are conspicuous by their absence.

The Puerto Rican clergy now contain many Americans, who have replaced the Spanish. Until recently, no native Puerto Rican was a member of the Church hierarchy. The middle and upper strata which once looked to Spain for their identification now look toward the United States. In the business world most Puerto Ricans in positions of importance either work directly for American firms or are indirectly dependent on American businesses. There are a few in the upper strata who strive to maintain their Spanish identification. But it is widely acknowledged that Puerto Ricans who wish to be "successful" or to hold middle-class jobs should emphasize their American traits and speech and deemphasize their Puerto Rican qualities.

These factors have created a sense of self-hatred among the Puerto Ricans. A cultural and psychic hierarchy has been established with things and values Puerto Rican at the bottom and American ones at the top. American norms and values have been internalized as the standards by which Puerto Ricans evaluate themselves. To be modern, to be fashionable, and to be socially successful is to be as American as possible.

The self-hatred that emanates from this syndrome manifests itself in different ways. As consumers, Puerto Ricans purchase American-made goods even when equivalent island-made products are available at the same or lower price. Puerto Rican goods have had such a negative image that Puerto Rican manufacturers give English rather than Spanish names to their products in hopes of increasing their sales. The situation became so noticeable in 1965 that the Puerto Rican government hired an advertising agency to improve the image of the goods produced on the island. Self-hatred is also revealed in areas more crucial than buying habits. Alcoholism rates are reported to be among the world's highest. The drug addiction rate is about one addict for every 250 island residents. The suicide and accident rates are also significant. In short, analogous to the experience of the American Negro and Indian, the Puerto Rican has learned to hate himself for being a Puerto Rican and for not being an American.

This cycle of self-hatred, however, is being broken among certain Puerto Ricans and the militance and violence of recent years may be viewed as a direct consequence of this. The hatred is now beginning to be directed outward. Frantz Fanon, William H. Grier and Price M. Cobbs argue that as a colonial people begin to free themselves from the external and internal forces, the focus on their hostility shifts from themselves to their oppressors. The intensity of the violence is related to the degree to which a people has learned to hate itself. For these authors, outwardly directed violence is not only a consequence of psychological oppression but a sign of health. Accepting this thesis, what intervened to break the cycle of self-hatred among segments of the Puerto Rican populace?

Increasingly, as Puerto Ricans came into closer contact with Americans on the mainland and on the island, they learned that regardless of what they considered themselves, Americans generally thought of them as Puerto Ricans. Those who believed themselves to be bona fide Americans had their identity claim rudely challenged. They were not defined as Americans but as Puerto Ricans, which in the American hierarchy of prejudice meant being slightly better than a Negro. The experience has proved to be particularly embittering for the young and the better educated. Pedro

Albizu Campos, the fiery leader of the now defunct Puerto Rican Nationalist party, developed his hatred for the United States at Harvard and in the U.S. Army. Indeed, according to Gordon Lewis, a professor at the UPR and author of *Puerto Rico: Freedom and Power in the Caribbean*, experience in the U.S. Army has made the Puerto Rican ex-GIs among the most bitter anti-Americans on the island. Greater awareness of American attitudes in addition to personal contact has helped to provoke a more militant Puerto Rican spirit.

The massive presence of the American mass media in Puerto Rico brought to the Puerto Ricans throughout the sixties the vivid story of the Negro struggle in the United States. The shift from the Civil Rights Movement of the early 1960s to the Black Power Movement of the last few years was not lost upon the younger Puerto Ricans. The daily lessons witnessed on the television screens began to strike responsive chords; the coverage of ethnic groups in the United States proudly proclaiming their heritage gave the Puerto Ricans a positive role model.

So too was the student rebellion, both black and white, brought into the Puerto Rican consciousness. The youth began to absorb and emulate the messages, the themes and the tactics of their American counterparts. Contacts were developed between Puerto Rican youth and SNCC and SDS. On January 26, 1967, Stokley Carmichael as the official representative of SNCC signed a "protocol of co-operation" with the President of FUPI. In this protocol, SNCC fomally recognized FUPI as an equal and an ally in the common struggle against American imperialism.

Ironically, even the American liberal heritage proved to be a factor causing the Puerto Ricans, and again particularly the better educated ones, to reexamine their Puerto Rican identities. They learned to apply the American ideals and values to which they were exposed in their classrooms and by the media to their own experience and to their own island. American texts and media lauded the principle of national self-determination. American colonists were heroes who had justly fought for their country's independence despite the fact that the people against whom they fought spoke the same language, had the same religions, and shared in their cultural tradition. Woodrow Wilson had nobly committed the United States to the support of peoples struggling for their national existence. World War II had been fought to defend nations from powerful aggressors and to free those who had already come under their yoke. In the post-war era, the United States had looked favorably upon the colonies of Europe breaking away from their mother countries. Both the Korean and Vietnamese Wars were officially depicted as efforts by America to ensure that these Asian peoples would have the right to determine their own national existence free from foreign domination. For many Puerto Ricans the inevitable question was: "Why shouldn't this historic ideal of America apply to Puerto Rico as well as Vietnam or Korea?"

The Vietnam War and the draft have also contributed to the rise of militancy in Puerto Rico, just as they have in the United States. Large segments of draft-age and college-age youth, similar to their counterparts on the mainland, question the morality, the methods and the purpose of the War. They also object to being drafted to fight in such a struggle. For many, anti-Americanism is the equivalent to the anti-government or anti-establishment attitude of American youth who oppose the War. However, there is an ingredient in the situation which is unique to Puerto Rico. The Vietnam War lends itself to characterization as a foreign war, a war that really doesn't seem relevant to the needs or interests of Puerto Ricans. There is also resentment over the fact that they are being drafted by a government in which Puerto Ricans are barred from any official representation. Puerto Ricans are eligible for the draft as citizens, but unlike other citizens they cannot vote for President, Senator or Congressman. The continuation of the draft and the Vietnam War, as well as the emotions aroused by the sentencing of an increasing number of Puerto Ricans who refuse induction, have contributed to the radicalization of many Puerto Ricans. These same factors also give the Puerto Rican militants an important issue and have placed in their hand a lever with which to move the islanders toward independence.

Another factor that has alienated Puerto Ricans from the United States and raised the level of hostile feelings is the presence of approximately 50,000 Cuban emigres on the island. These emigres were encouraged to come to an already overcrowded Puerto Rico by the United States government. Here again was another official act in which the Puerto Ricans had no voice. Furthermore, the Cubans have proved themselves to be shrewd and hard-driving businessmen. Within a short period of time, they have moved into positions of prominence in different sectors of the Puerto Rican economy. At the same time, the Cubans have made little effort to hide their disdain for the Puerto Ricans. One Cuban refugee, after first introducing himself to me by name, quickly continued: "I am a Cuban, not a Puerto Rican. I work."

Also, despite their recent arrival to the island, the Cubans have not hesitated to become involved in politics. They are militantly anti-Communist and many view any movement for Puerto Rican independence as a Communist plot. Some have organized themselves into a clandestine "Cuban Power" organization to combat Communism and the independence movement with more than just speeches. Conversely, they are ardent supporters of statehood, for they see it as the only way to ensure that the island will remain in American hands. (This is a case of history repeating itself. In the nineteenth century, as Latin Americans freed themselves from Spain, the defeated loyalists made their way to Puerto Rico. They too quickly occupied important positions and were hostile to any Puerto Rican movement that threatened to weaken Puerto Rico's ties with the mother country.) Obviously, the Cubans are not a stabilizing factor in Puerto Rican politics.

The portents for the future in Puerto Rico are not bright. Many issues and problems underlying the rise in militancy are deeply rooted in the history and social structure of the island. As such, they are not amenable to an easy or a quick solution. For too long both Puerto Ricans and Americans have avoided facing the most basic issue in Puerto Rican politics. The rise in the level of militance and violence is symbolic of a society that is preparing, after many years, to come to grips with important problems and its national essence.

The Death of Dolores

OSCAR LEWIS

In June, 1963, when I began my study of her family, Dolores Corrado was 36 years old. She lived in the San Juan slum I have called La Esmeralda, in a flimsy two-room shack at the edge of the sea; there was an ever-present danger of being swept away by high waves. Dolores had bought the little house for $450 with money she won in the lottery. She used the rest of her winnings to install electricity, running water, a tiny toilet, a refrigerator, and a few pieces of shabby second-hand furniture. Dolores lived with her fourth husband, Arturo, her nine-year-old son Millo, of a previous marriage, her mother Doña Carmen and a young man, Araceli, who was a boarder.

Dolores had formerly been the economic mainstay of her mother and son, but she was now too ill to work. The *family income was very meagre and sporadic. Arturo, who often disappeared for days, would give Dolores a few pesos now and then. Millo's earnings as a shoeshine boy at that time rarely exceeded a dollar or two a day. Doña Carmen had a steady but small income of $7.50 a month from relief, and Araceli, who contributed only when he was working, gave just enough to pay for his food and for Dolores' daily supply of cigarettes and beer.*

From the tender age of six or seven, Dolores had worked as a coffee-picker, a charcoal burner, and a domestic servant in the hill country of Jayuya. She never attended school and was still illiterate. At age 15 she left the country for San Juan, where she worked as a housemaid and a kitchen helper until age 21, when she became pregnant and was married. Abandoned by her husband after the birth of her second child, Dolores went back to work, but was unable to hold a job because of severe asthma attacks. When she and her mother and children were on the verge of starvation, she took up prostitution.

Dolores was pretty and spirited but the harsh experience of her profession, the death of a son, and her own explosive, violently self-destructive personality, undermined her health. When I met her, she was pale, emaciated, almost bedridden and obviously very ill. She was an erratic informant, but when she felt well she told her story with enjoyment and with lively humor. Dolores died of tuberculosis five months after my last interview with her.

The following excerpt is from my forthcoming book, Six Women: A Study of Three Generations in a Puerto Rican Family. *It is narrated by Magdalena, the eldest of Doña Carmen's five daughters.*

From my house I could look down the alleyway to the left and see Lola's house. I used to watch her sitting by

her window, looking out at the sea. When she left the sanatorium in April she promised to return, but she never did.
She stayed home with her son Millo and was taking her
medicine, and after about a month she began to feel a little
better. She had been to the public health clinic a few times
and told *mamá* that she had another appointment in July.
She had hopes of being cured. Of course, she did!

CAST OF CHARACTERS

Doña Carmen	*age 71*	The mother
Dolores (Lola)	*age 39*	
Eva	*age 30*	
Alicia	*age 28*	Daughters of Doña Carmen
Sofía	*age 26*	
Magdalena	*age 42*	
Esteban	*age 47*	Magdalena's husband
Arturo Hoyos	*age 44*	Dolores's husband
Chango	*age 28*	Alicia's husband
Antonio	*age 26*	Sofía's husband
Robert	*age 14*	
Danny	*age 11*	Magdalena's sons
Carlitos	*age 9*	
Millo	*age 11*	Dolores's son

Lola's husband, Arturo Hoyos, hadn't shown up for
over a month. He was living with another woman, and the
only reason Lola wasn't short of money was because Millo
brought her what he earned by shining shoes. Why, that
boy brought her seven or eight dollars a day. Every single
day! Think of it! She forced him to bring her all that
money. I'd say to her, "Forgive me, *comai* (my friend),

but it isn't right to make the kid bring you so much. You know a shoeshine boy can't earn more than two or three dollars a day, even if he kills himself working. It's us mothers who are to blame when a child steals, because if I tell my sons, 'Unless you bring me such-and-such an amount of money, I'll kill you,' the kid will do anything to save his skin."

Lola's answer to that was, "Ah, let him steal. Let him do whatever he pleases! Better he should hold up a bank than bring me a few measly dollars. Money, lots of money, that's what I want!"

Lola needed money to pay for her vices. She drank a dollar's worth of beer every day, besides a pint of rum with anise which cost another seventy-five cents. She'd also give me a dollar or two a day to cook for her kid, as well as for mine.

On the Monday before Mother's Day, comai Lola wasn't feeling too good, but she joked and teased as usual. After kidding around for a while, she said she wanted a mango, the real meaty kind they call "bull's balls." It was a craving she had, I guess. I managed to get one for her and she ate every bit of it. Later that week she even ate some chopped ham.

Mamá visited Lola a lot. She was living with my sister Sofía and her husband Antonio, and they were only a four or five minute walk from Lola's house. On Mother's Day in the morning, mamá went to take Lola some pigeon broth. Lola didn't have a gift for her so she said, "Mami, there's some soap and a bottle of perfume on the shelf. Take them, they're too sweet and the smell makes me sick." Mamá pretended not to hear and went right on talking. When she went away she left the things there. By then Lola was looking better; she was expecting me to come over with a cup of coffee. But before I got there, along came that husband of hers, drinking beer. He said, "I'd like to smash this bottle in your face, but rather than land in jail for just hurting you, I might as well kill you and have done with it. Anybody with TB should be killed." Then he pulled out a gun and put it up against Lola's head, saying, "Look, here's my gift to you!" Lola screamed, "Dear God, help me!" Then Arturo wheeled around and took a shot at the electric light cables in front of the house. Lola begged him to stop because he might start a fire and burn us all to death. Arturo told her, "As long as I save my own skin, you and your family can go fuck yourselves and shit on your mother because you're nothing but a bunch of no-good whores."

Lola said to him, "Go ahead, Arturo, sink half the world if you like—you'll get pulled into jail before you know how you got there."

"Is that right?" he said, "Then I might as well kill you first."

"You aren't man enough to kill me," said Lola, and she began to cry. She cried and cried like a Mary Magdalene. Arturo was gone when I came, and Lola said, "Comai, Arturo is giving me a bad time and God only knows how I'm going to defend myself. I wish I could kill that man!" When Millo came back from shining shoes and saw her crying he went to mamá's house looking for a weapon to kill Arturo.

Arturo showed up at mamá's first with a story about how he'd offered Lola three dollars and she had refused it, saying she wasn't a beggar. While he was speaking, Millo came in and Arturo started backing down the stairs as soon as he caught sight of the boy. Millo made signs to mamá, asking for a knife. Mamá said to Arturo, "All right, *compai* (my friend), with your permission, I can't stand here making conversation with you any longer. You've no call to come gossiping about a sick woman who doesn't bother you nor anybody else either."

"Oh, never mind," Arturo answered, "I won't be talking anymore because I'm going."

"I won't miss you any," mamá said.

I stayed with Lola until she got over her crying spell. When Millo came back I left. But she must have cried again that night because in the morning, after Esteban got up to go to work, Millo called to me that she was coughing up blood. What I think is that Arturo's behavior brought on the haemoptysis.

When I got there, comai Lola was crouching over the basin which was already half full of blood. I helped her stand up and get into bed. She was in pretty bad shape.

I went over to Sofía's to tell mamá about Lola. Mamá was doing the dishes when I arrived and I said, "Mamá, do you know why I came?"

"How would I know, child? Can it be to tell me Lola is dead?"

"She had an attack of haemoptysis last night that practically finished her."

Mamá said, "Ay, Dios," and she ran to Lola's house.

I had to go back home and get my boys off to school but I went over to Lola's every little while to rub her chest with bay rum. That was the only thing to do because she had a bad pain in the chest and could hardly breathe. By evening she was better.

On Tuesday I had to take my son Robert to the Puerta de Tierra clinic because he'd been having the earache so bad that he hadn't let me get any sleep for three nights. I was waiting for Robert's turn at the clinic when compai Ismael came in and told me that Lola had gotten another attack of haemoptysis and was all alone. I phoned Chango, Alicia's husband, at the La Esmeralda dispensary and asked him to send word to mamá that Lola was very sick and that she should go stay with her until I could get there.

I had to wait a long time at the clinic for Robert's turn, but when I got to Lola's, mamá was sitting by the bed fanning her. Lola was gasping and choking and too weak to get up. "Look, child," mamá said to her, "you know that when someone's sick in bed, whether they are getting better or worse, they should have a priest."

"But there's no one to fetch one for me."

"I'm ready to do it," said mamá. So she went right away and got a priest at a church over in Tanca Street. He said, "I'll come at about four."

Antonio, Sofía, and Alicia arrived while the priest was there. He asked everybody to clear out so Lola could confess her sins. Then he rubbed Holy Oil on her but he said he couldn't give her communion because of the blood she was spitting. After the priest left, Lola told me, "Comai, the first thing I spoke about to the priest were the quarrels you and I had, because it would hurt too much to go without being forgiven by you."

"I have always forgiven you," I said, "and, anyway, you're going to last longer than me." But she answered, "No, I'm dying. The one I want to see is comai Eva."

Lola seemed to get better later so mamá went home. That night, around ten, Lola had a lot of visitors, mostly people who came to say goodbye to her. Her little boy, Millo, being sort of wrong in the head like he is, was jumping and dancing around in the crowd while she coughed up blood, as if seeing his mother like that made him happy.

All of a sudden Lola let out a yell, "Ayyy, I'm choking!" We brought her a basin to spit into and then right away we had to bring another to put under the first one. We had to keep changing basins because Lola coughed up so much blood she fairly emptied herself out. Right in the middle of everything she begged us to send for Eva. She was white as a sheet. My husband Esteban was holding her up but he was drunk and pressed her real hard to help her get the blood out. He only made her choke more and I made him change places with me. But first I had to wipe Lola's blood from his arms. The bleeding wouldn't stop and I got blood on my hands too. I wasn't afraid though— why should I be afraid of my own sister? Lola finally fell back in my arms, fainting. For more than an hour she leaned against my left shoulder. She looked dead, completely dead; cold, as if she'd been put on ice. I got icy cold myself, holding her.

When Lola came to, the first thing she did was beg us to send for Eva. She wanted to be forgiven for having married Arturo, who was her compai and Eva's ex-husband. Sofía rushed home like a madwoman to get some money from mamá to send a cablegram to New York asking Eva to come. Mamá gave her the money but the cablegram was returned because we put the wrong address on it. So then Antonio wrote out the address on an envelope and sent her a letter instead.

Lola was getting worse. I couldn't take care of her myself because I can't lose my sleep at night. There was no extra bed in her house and I'd have to sleep on the floor. Besides, I have kids to take care of. With so many thieves and criminals around, I was afraid someone might break into my house to steal and maybe even hurt the kids or something. I said mamá could stay with Lola, but Alicia and Sofía wouldn't hear of it! They said, "If mamá stays we'll wind up with two corpses on our hands." So we asked Lola if she wanted us to take her to Alicia's house. "If that's where you want me to go, I'm willing," she said. Antonio picked her up and carried her all the way there in his arms. They sat up with her until midnight, then mamá took over and watched her till morning.

Lola said to mamá, "Listen, you and I have a promise to fulfill; I'm going to take you with me when I die."

"Yes, I remember and I'm expecting you to keep your word," mamá said.

Seven nights they took turns like that, so there was always someone awake and looking after her until daybreak. I couldn't take care of her but as long as she was at Alicia's house, I kept visiting her. She would lie there chatting with us as if nothing had happened, but every time she coughed, she spat out blood by the mouthful. And when she saw Alicia working so hard in the house she gave her money to send out the ironing. She said, "I won't live long enough to eat my way through this money, anyway. My days are numbered."

One night when mamá was sitting with her, Lola said, "Mamá, get somebody to write down on a paper for me to sign that I'm leaving the house to my son. Then sell it and put the money into the bank for him." But nobody who could do it showed up.

Then Lola got it into her head that she wanted to take the boy with her. She'd say to him, "Damn you, I'm going to take you with me. Come and stand here beside me so I can kill you!" She tried to bribe Alicia's little girl to bring her a knife. She said she didn't want to leave Millo an orphan and risk his turning into a thief. But Alicia sent Millo to school and told Lola to ask God's forgiveness and to beg Him for strength to leave her son behind.

On Thursday her husband Arturo showed up. He was standing just outside the front door and when Lola heard his voice, she said, "Don't let him in, Alicia." So, when Arturo asked, Alica said, "No, Lola doesn't want you here."

"I'm not all that bad," he said.

"It's you that brought this illness upon her, threatening her with a gun," Alicia said.

Arturo denied it, "Say what you like," he said, "but it's still a lie. I never pulled a gun on her."

Then mamá told him, "Never again will you be allowed to set foot in this house. As long as you live you have no right to come here. You and I have a little quarrel to settle; the time will come when we'll have it out."

"There's no time like the present," said Arturo, "but suit yourself." So they left it at that.

Eva arrived from New York on Saturday and she and Lola fell into each other's arms. Eva was weeping and wailing, "Ay, comai Lola of my soul!" Lola threw herself on the floor and groveled like a worm until we picked her up and laid her on the sofa again. Ay, bendito (Oh, Jesus!), it was pitiful.

Lola had two more attacks there at Alicia's. After the first one, she got better. According to mamá, she began to joke again. She'd smile and say, "Ay, mamá, you've got a face like a cunt!" Sick as she was, she was happy and good humored. On Monday she was terribly upset because of a complaint that Millo had been stealing.

Millo had a little silver hand, the kind they call the Hand of God, that he said he'd bought at Santos' store for a quarter. A few days later, he brought home a good gold ring. He kept bringing home things like that. Then one day, while he was shining shoes at the docks, a man who had an office there caught sight of the silver hand and called a cop: He said a little hand like that and several other things were missing from his office.

Millo didn't give the cop his right address because of Lola and took him to his godmother's house instead. But the cop said, no, that wouldn't do, and Millo had to take him home. When Lola heard what had happened, she said, "It's you cops who are to blame for kids growing up to be thieves and drug addicts because if a mother beats up her child you arrest her and make her pay a fine. So how can you expect a mother to correct her children?"

"You can kill the kid and eat him, for all I care," the cop answered. At that, Lola got up, grabbed a stick and tried to beat Millo, but she was too tired and sick. She got an asthma attack and had to lie down again. The asthma brought on another hemorrhage. She cried out, "Ay, mamá," and she died there, in mamá's arms. But our screams and wails brought her back. Eva kept bawling, "Dear God, don't take my sister away. Oh, sister of my heart." That's what brought the woman back. Lola opened her eyes, looked all around, and said, "I can't go; I can't go." Twice, like that. It was us sisters crying that wouldn't let her go in peace! What we did was make her so desperate that she couldn't go through her change.

Alicia said, "Eva hasn't pardoned comai Lola, that's what's keeping her there on that bed!" Eva wanted to pardon Lola just before she went back to New York but Alicia said Lola wasn't going to last that long. "The only thing that's keeping her alive is that she wants your forgiveness." Eva went to ask her mother-in-law, Bertha, her opinion. Bertha said to her, "If Alicia advises it, you'd better do it." Eva still didn't believe it, so she went to the priest. He said, "I've done all I can so that the Lord would receive your sister in His arms. Now you should pardon her as Alicia advises."

So Eva went to Lola and asked her, "Comai, is it my forgiveness you are waiting for?" Lola opened her eyes wide and said, "That's what I'm waiting for." Then Eva knelt and pressed her hand and said, "Comai, you are forgiven." Lola couldn't speak after that. She lost her voice.

When I left that night, Lola was in a bad way. She couldn't swallow anything, not even water. Mami would say, "Child, would you like some water?" and she'd make signs that she wanted mami to moisten her mouth with a bit of wet cotton. Mamá kept on doing that until the spirit came down to Lola about half past eight it was, and she sat up in her bed. That brought on a fit of coughing and spitting blood. She coughed so hard that she fell off the bed. Then, with the blood running from her mouth, she screamed, "Ay, a taxi, a taxi! Take me to the hospital. I don't want to die here. Mami, don't be so tight. There's money here!" After having spent so much, Lola still had forty dollars under her mattress.

Antonio flew to get a taxi while the others stayed with Lola. She kind of said goodbye to them then. Millo was hanging about, near the door, and Lola beckoned to him. She kissed him and gave him a long look, as if saying, "This is the last time I'll ever see him."

Antonio came back and said he had a taxi waiting. He took her in his arms, just as she was, in nothing but a nightgown, and carried her up to the Boulevard.

At the hospital they took Lola to the ward and mamá, Eva, Sofía, and Antonio went with her. The doctor ordered the nurse to give her two bottles of serum but after about fifteen minutes he touched her and said, "Take the serum away." By that time, her skin was punctured all over from so many injections. But she felt strong enough to talk and told the doctor, "Those tubes in my nose are choking me to death." So the doctor had them taken away, the oxygen too. "She's done for," he said.

"Done for? What a thing to say!" mamá protested. That made the doctor get into an argument with her. Finally he told the nurse, "Take out the old lady and the girl." After mamá and Sofía left, he said to Antonio, "She's got about half an hour more to live." Antonio rushed out of the room crying. Mamá began to scream and Eva was screaming like crazy too. The doctor came and gave them an injection to quiet them down. "We are women, all of us," Antonio said, "because the old lady is crying, comai is crying, and I'm crying too, I'm too tender-hearted to take it."

When they said goodbye to Lola, she begged them, "Take good care of Millo for me," and then, "Mami, a kiss for each of you."

"Don't worry," mamá told her, "think of God and the Virgin Mary. They are the ones you should turn to now, not anybody here on earth. May God and the Virgin forgive you for the wrong you have done and forgive all those who have wronged you." They went away then, still weeping but feeling much calmer because of the injections. That night mamá couldn't sleep. She was up before anyone else. Then she got a note from the sanatorium saying, "Urgent, for the relatives of Dolores Figueroa."

"That must mean she's dead," Sofía told mamá, "because if it was to ask for a blood donor or something, they would have sent another kind of note."

Mamá went over to the dispensary to call the hospital and they told her that Lola was on the list of the dead and that some member of the family should go there and get her. Mamá rushed back home like a madwoman. When she told Antonio he acted crazy too, sticking his feet into his bedroom slippers without looking, and putting on a dirty shirt and rushing out like that.

When they told Millo his mother was dead, he cried and screamed. He rushed outside and they went after him and found him all stiff, like his nerves were all twisted up. He was crying, "My mami's dead, mami's dead . . . what will become of me now?" Mamá said to him, "Don't worry, son, no matter what anybody says, I'm here and you can count on me."

I had been sleeping and didn't know anything about Lola's death that morning until Millo came and I heard him ask Rafael García, "Is Auntie there?"

"Yes, she is."

"Tell her that mami died, will you?"

That kid didn't seem to have any feelings at all about anything. He said 'Mami died' as calmly as if she'd been no relative of his. I was paralyzed when I heard the news, because of that nervous illness of mine. Not one tear came at the moment. I just started trembling and trembling, but after the first sob, I cried so hard that Rafael said, "If you keep on crying like that, I'll go back home and leave your house with nobody to take care of it. What you should do is go over there." But I couldn't go yet because I didn't have a black dress to wear. I sent my boy to borrow one for me and he didn't get back until after three.

Eva went to shop for some clothes to bury Lola in and she took Millo with her. When he came back he asked mamá, "Grandma, will they bury mami soon? I'm going to New York with auntie."

Mamá asked Eva, "Did you tell him that?"

"Yes, I asked him to go with me."

Mamá said to her, "Well, daughter, that's your lookout. You know that he isn't what you'd call a good boy, but he isn't a bad boy either. He's a little of both." She wanted to keep Millo but Antonio didn't like to have him around because of Ruby. The two of them are like wasps, they fight all the time. So, it was better to have Millo in New York. What the eyes don't see, the heart doesn't feel. If someone hit him up there, he could hit back. He was big enough now.

About one o'clock in the afternoon Antonio returned from the hospital and told mamá that they already did an autopsy on Lola and that we had to buy her a coffin. So each of us went around to collect money. It was the only thing I could do for Lola after she died. I collected very little, about six-fifty or seven dollars, from neighbors and from friends in San Juan. I couldn't walk much because ever since Lola had leaned against my shoulder when she was sick, my legs swelled up and my whole left side felt numb. But with the money I bought a large tin of crackers, a pound of coffee, two pounds of sugar and half a cheese, and sent it all to Alicia's house.

Antonio wrote out a paper asking the neighbors to help pay for the funeral and Alicia sent her husband Chango to show it around and collect some money. The people who read the paper began to joke about it. They said that the lady hadn't really died but had made up that story herself to raise money to buy rum. Chango answered that the paper said plain as plain that she was dead. So then they told him to go and get the money from Doña Felisa, the mayoress. Chango had to control himself because those people were all acting disrespectful to comai Lola and to Millo, saying the kid was a thief. Chango said they could do just as they pleased, but they were all invited to come and see the dead woman if they had any doubts. Then he went back home, mad as anything.

Millo kept asking him to go out to raise more money, but Chango said no, he wasn't going to be embarrassed like that again. Millo asked Arturo for money and Arturo came crying and making a fool of himself. He had no call to be weeping like a hypocrite, when he was the one that killed Dolores. He ran off to rent a niche in the churchyard for her and didn't show up again until that night, when he came in beating his breast.

He asked Alicia for permission to bring his wife. "Never!" she said, "That wife of yours is as much your mistress as comai Lola was. If you come to the wake with her, people will talk."

They didn't let Arturo go to the wake and he came to my house looking for me. He told me, "I just had to go to Lola's house. I still love her."

"But you didn't know how to keep her love," I said. "The truth is, you didn't love her. If you had been a man of dignity and worthy of respect, you would not have abandoned her, no matter how she talked and quarreled with you. Knowing she was sick, you should have let her tongue run on and not paid any attention. You would have stuck by your wife, and then she could have died in your arms, under your care." When he heard that, Arturo burst into tears. He pulled out his handkerchief, wiped his eyes, and walked out.

Later that afternoon Antonio and mamá went to Morovis to get a *rezador* (one who prays) to lead the prayers at the wake. He wanted ten dollars but they paid him five. They told him they couldn't lay their hands on any more money. He stayed all night, praying.

They brought Lola from the hospital to Alicia's house and laid her out there. Four people carried her coffin and one person got underneath and lifted it up. According to mamá everybody was crying, but when I got there at three-thirty, my sisters looked perfectly calm and happy. Mamá had her head bent but she wasn't crying. I saw Lola there in her coffin and that's when I really cried. She looked as beautiful as the Virgin Mary because they had made up her face. She looked real young, absolutely lovely, like an image of the Virgin. Oh, that's when I really cried, remembering all the fights we'd had and all we had been through together and our games and jokes and everything It broke my heart and wrung my soul to see her go like she did.

They had taken a photo of her lying there, and another with mamá, Sofía, Alicia, and Millo standing beside the coffin. Then Antonio came and said they shouldn't have opened the box because the infection was shut up inside it, but mamá told him the more one tried to protect oneself, the quicker one caught the infection. It's true. After all, everyone of us has worn clothes left by cousins who had died of the chest sickness like Lola, yet, thank God, we all came out all right.

It made me sad to see that Millo didn't feel his mother's death any more than if she had been a stranger to him. And to think that all her worries and sorrow had been over leaving him! She kept begging mamá and me to take good care of the child and look after him. Yet there was Millo, laughing and dancing and joking with Alicia's little girls. The oldest girl said, "Don't act like that. You've just lost your mother and you shouldn't be happy."

"Oh, I still have grandmother," he answered, and Alicia came right back at him and said, "Well, your grandmother is going the same way your mother went, so quit horsing around. Show more respect and be sad for a while."

The way that kid acted! He's crazy or something. He was so happy over the trip to New York that Eva had cooked up for him. He kept repeating, "Ay, how wonderful, I'm going to New York!" as if Lola hadn't meant a thing to him. Some of us suspect (we wouldn't dream of mentioning this to mamá) that maybe the child wasn't too fond of his mother because she treated him pretty badly. The black and blue marks from her last beating were still on him, may God forgive her. Lola had such a long, boring illness, you see, that she took it out on the kid.

As long as she lived, Lola had friends but after she was dead there wasn't anybody to speak of who went to see her.

I didn't stay long at the wake because I wasn't feeling well. Only mamá and my sisters were there to pray the rosaries all night. Everybody else stayed away; they left her alone, absolutely alone—she, who had had so many friends in San Juan! Not even her husband was there.

Everything went smoothly until around 5 A.M. when a gang of boys came in and began making jokes about the corpse. They'd run in yelling, "Catch 'em, corpse!" and then run out again, laughing. When Alicia had all she could take she said, "Those boys don't deserve to be treated with respect. I'm going to tell them off." So she stood up and yelled, "What do you think this is, a ball? If you guys are scared of the dead, stay away from wakes. Don't come here and interrupt our prayers with your horseplay!" After that, they all went away.

For the funeral I rented a car for those who were to go with me. My car was full. Cheo, the *comisario de barrio* (justice of the peace), came to represent the Popular Party and he took some people in his car. The man next door to mamá did too. There were five cars in all, costing ten dollars each. We all rode behind the hearse to Monacillo cemetery. Bebo is buried there too.

At the cemetery mamá didn't cry out loud. She just stood there, with the tears running down her face. She is a sick woman; she suffers from heart trouble. But mamá even tried to comfort me saying, "Don't cry child, that will only give Lola more pain." But when we got to the grave, I don't know . . . I was carrying a wreath in one hand and was leading my youngest child with the other and suddenly my hands were empty without my having noticed who took the wreath or the child.

When they were lowering Lola into the grave and taking more photographs, mamá cried out, "Ay, my child, you promised to take me with you but you didn't. You abandoned me and left me here in this world." And then she fell down in a fit. None of the people there had the courage to grab hold of her except me. I was nervous anyway and couldn't cry, so I grabbed her to keep her from falling. But my own mind failed, too, and I didn't realize what was going on. Why, I didn't even see when they covered Lola with earth. They gave mamá an injection and put me into the car I had hired.

After that mamá didn't feel a thing. She saw things happen and nothing seemed to matter to her. She didn't even know how the burial went. That night Antonio hired a car to take Eva and Millo to the airport and mamá didn't notice that either. It was only later that she was told Eva had to go right back because she's on relief and wasn't supposed to be away from New York.

In the end, it was Antonio who paid the expenses with money he had saved in the bank to buy a house. He even went and bought Millo a plane ticket to New York because Eva was broke; she had gotten her own ticket on credit. Antonio is only a brother-in-law but he paid for everything. According to what they told me, the coffin and everything cost over two hundred dollars. He's still paying the installments to the funeral parlor but mamá is paying him back for the coffin by renting out Lola's house for $15 a month and turning over the money to him.

Arturo stayed away for three whole days after Lola was buried. That's how bad he is. Then he got high on beer and came over to see mamá. He said to her, "You've been going around saying I only gave three dollars for Lola's funeral. I gave twenty-five."

Mamá said to him, "Well, maybe you did start out with twenty-five but all I got was three. You must have been playing with yourself on the way over and got your fingers so sticky that the rest of the money stuck to your fist."

"Now look, if it comes to that, how do I know you didn't pinch it yourself?"

"You miserable thief!" said mamá, "you're the one who steals, not me. You steal over at the docks. I never go to the docks and I've got a clean record everywhere." Then she called Alicia. "Alicia, how much money did compai Arturo hand over to me in front of Chango and you?"

"Three dollars," she said.

"You stole the rest between you," Arturo yelled. Alicia is a redhead and has a temper to match. She flared up and grabbed Chango's policeman's billy and started to call Arturo names . . . *cabrón*, (cuckold) good-for-nothing, pitiful-excuse-of-a-man, and a few others as well. It's a good thing Arturo didn't try to hit her. He just said, "Oh, shut up! I don't want to get mixed up in any more quarrels with you people. Just tell me whether you want friendliness or unfriendliness between you and me."

"Unfriendliness!" mamá said. "What do we want your dirty friendship for?" Mamá swears she's going to get even with Arturo someday, that as long as they both live, there's a quarrel between them. Mamá told him she hoped he dropped dead.

Then he came wandering around near Lola's house, like a stray mongrel puppy. But he got kind of fresh with me, touching my face and so on, so I told him off too. I said, "The dead woman is my sister and I at least, may God forgive her, respect my *compadres* (fellowmen). So stop fooling around, see?" I haven't been bothered by him since.

I don't know about my sisters, but as for myself, I seemed to have lost my mind in those days. I was in such a state of mind that once I took a bottle of water to put in the refrigerator and instead I stuck it among the clothes in that rickety old thing we call a wardrobe. My mind still wanders, and I still hear Lola. I hear her laughing and joking and whistling to me. My kids, too, say they hear and see her all the time. And when I'm going to do something, Lola's the first person I mention. Like the other day, I made plantain dumplings and, meaning to send some to comai Sofía, I said to Danny, "Here, take this to comai Lola. I have Lola on my mind. And that's the way it goes."

Mamá began saying that the dead don't come back because Lola's had plenty of time to appear and so far she hasn't. Mamá swears she hasn't heard any noises even. She went to a spiritist who told her, "Your daughter is full of life. She's happy and grateful because her little boy went to New York." So mamá is calmer about her now.

But I am not at ease about comai Lola because it seems to me she is still suffering. She owes a month, or maybe two, on her vow to wear Our Lady of Carmel's habit and I think Lola wants me to pay the Virgin by wearing the habit myself. Last night I had a kind of revelation about it. I dreamed that mamá had brought in the can of slop for the pigs while I was watching television. As she passed, I grabbed a piece of fatback that was on top and I began to chew on it. Suddenly I saw Lola at the window, with her arms crossed on the sill, just like she used to do. She says to me, "What a slop you are, eating that fatback from the pigs' dinner!" I said, "Ah . . ." and then I couldn't get out another word. I was paralyzed and struck dumb, seeing her there, rubbing her eyes as if she just woke up. I made signs to mamá to come over, because my throat was completely paralyzed. I made signs to the neighbors too. Everybody saw Lola. I felt like laughing but Lola said, "Don't anybody laugh at me now or you'll see what I'll do to you!" She shut the window quickly, got down and walked into my parlor. Then she tried to grab me, mamá, and Esteban by the legs. My neighbor, Doña Laura, said to her, "Now look here, don't do that. You are dead now. If you keep this up you will kill your sister and mother and brother-in-law. Can't you see that you are a dead woman?"

"Ah, that's what you think," Lola said, "I'm not a bit dead. I'm more alive than any of you!" Then, suddenly, she stood up and ran into the bedroom in desperation. She yelled to my son, "Carlitos, come here. Carlitos, come here!" She wanted Carlitos to lift her nightgown and scratch her back. I said to her, "No, no! My little boy can't look at your back; you are dead. You're a ghost, so stop horsing around like that. You're only smoke and you shouldn't be coming here." At that she sort of evaporated. But later that night I felt as if somebody were touching me from head to foot.

I know my sister is not happy. I mean to go to a spiritist to find out if Lola wants me to pay off her vow to the

Virgin of Carmel. If I have to wear that habit for two months, I'll do it. I'll do that and anything more to bring her peace.

May 1969

NOTES ON CONTRIBUTORS

Anthony D. Fisher   "White Rites and Indian Rights"

Associate professor of anthropology and educational foundations at the University of Alberta, in Canada. He is co-editor of *The North American Indians: A Source Book*, and he has contributed articles about Canada's Indians to a number of Canadian journals.

Merwyn S. Gabarino   "Seminole Girl"

Assistant professor of anthropology at the University of Illinois at Chicago Circle, and a fieldworker in the Welfare and Family Services Department of the American Indian Center in Chicago.

Oscar Lewis   "The Death of Dolores"

Professor of anthropology at the University of Illinois. He has conducted family studies in Mexico, New York and Puerto Rico, and most recently in Cuba. Among his books are: *Five Families; The Children of Sanchez; Pedro Matinez: A Mexican Peasant and His Family;* and *La Vida: A Puerto Rican Family in the Culture of Poverty—San Juan and New York.*

Arthur Liebman   "The Puerto Rican Independence Movement"

Assistant professor of sociology at the State University of New York at Binghamton and a research fellow at Harvard University. He has published *The Politics of Puerto Rican Students* and has recently coauthored a monograph on Latin American students with Myron Glazer and Kenneth Walker.

Joseph L. Love   "*La Raza*: Mexican Americans in Rebellion"

Associate professor of history at University of Illinois, Urbana. He is the author of *Rio Grande do Sul and the Politics of Regionalism in Brazil*, (1970). He is presently working on a multi-authored, multi-volume study of regionalism in Brazil, 1889-1937.

Robert K. Thomas   "Renaissance and Repression: The Oklahoma Cherokee"

Associate professor at the Science of Society Division at Wayne State University. With Sol Tax, Thomas directed the Carnegie Cross-Cultural Education Project, which was primarily based upon the Cherokee Indians of Oklahoma.

Albert L. Wahrhaftig   "Renaissance and Repression: The Oklahoma Cherokee"

Assistant professor in the Division of Science and Society, Monteith College, Wayne State University. Wahrhaftig spent four years in the Cherokee Nation of Oklahoma, has done field work in Chiapas, Mexico, and was a Peace Corps Volunteer in Colombia. He has published articles in numerous social science journals.

Rosalie H. Wax   "The Warrior Dropouts"

Professor of anthropology at the University of Kansas. With Murray L. Wax she has published many works on American Indian education, and in 1969, a book on the changing ethos of the Vikings, *Magic, Fate and History*. She recently completed a book on anthropological field work.